National Defense Research Institute

ENLISTED PERSONNEL TRENDS IN THE SELECTED RESERVE, 1986–1994

Richard Buddin

Sheila Nataraj Kirby

Prepared for the Office of the Secretary of Defense

Approved for public release; distribution unlimited

RAND

PREFACE

This report presents the results of a study examining personnel readiness of the Selected Reserve Components from FY86–FY94. It describes the data, technical analyses, and findings in detail and will serve as a reference source for future work in this area. A companion report, MR-681/1-OSD, provides an executive summary of the study. It sets the findings in a policy context and points to some potential areas of concern with respect to reserve manning in the future.

The study builds on earlier work on reserve personnel readiness that was based on the FY89 inventory of reserve personnel and was reported in Grissmer et al. (1994a). That report highlighted a potential constraint to relying on the reserve force: the likelihood of future limits on the availability of experienced formerly active-duty personnel for reserve service resulting from the active drawdown.

The current study updates and extends the earlier analysis in a number of important ways. First, the data examined are more recent (through FY94) and reflect the early effects of both the active and the reserve drawdown; second, analyses of the large cohorts recently separated from active duty point to the success of the Reserve Components in recruiting from this prior-service pool; third, fears that Operation Desert Storm might lead to a huge outflow from the reserves can largely be laid to rest, as the analysis of attrition shows. Indeed, the study reveals that the Reserve Components have been remarkably successful in keeping quality high, attracting and retaining prior-service personnel, improving skill match rates at entry, and keeping attrition and skill-qualification rates fairly stable.

This work was sponsored by the Assistant Secretary for Reserve Affairs. This research was conducted in the Forces and Resources Policy Center, which is part of RAND's National Defense Research Institute, a federally funded research and development center sponsored by the Office of the Secretary of Defense, the Joint Staff, and the defense agencies.

CONTENTS

FIGURES

TABLES

SUMMARY

BACKGROUND

Changes in the personnel climate following Operation Desert Shield/Storm (ODS/S) have subjected the Selected Reserves to potentially conflicting demands. On the one hand, their strength is diminishing. The overall size of the reserves has declined nearly 15 percent, and the eventual target will reduce them 25 percent from their peak in FY89. At the same time, they will represent a larger fraction of the nation's defense—39 percent by FY99, up from 36 percent at the end of the Cold War.

On the other hand, indications are that the demand for the reserves will increase. They represent a major or sole source of a number of capabilities that could be important for contingencies in war or peace. For example, the Air Force Reserve provides half of the airlift crews; the Army Reserve has all the chemical brigades and heavy helicopter units, and about 70 percent of the medical assets; 90 percent of the cargo handling and shipping control falls under the purview of the Naval Reserve; and one of four Marine divisions is in the Marine Corps Reserve. Many of these capabilities could prove necessary in peacekeeping or humanitarian operations as well as in combat.

Against this backdrop of declining strength and increasing demands, policymakers have expressed concerns about the ability of the Selected Reserves to sustain themselves and remain responsive to the nation's security needs. One concern pertains to ODS/S's effect on the reserves' ability to attract new members. Does the activation of substantial numbers of the reserves bode ill for recruiting and retention? Other concerns relate to the ability of the reserves to attract experienced people. All other things being equal, prior-service personnel bring a wealth of experience and, if placed in a position that draws on their active-duty skill, can increase readiness and decrease training costs significantly. Recognizing the contribution of prior-service personnel to readiness, Congress has directed the Army National Guard to raise the prior-service content of its enlisted force to 65 percent. But the active forces are drawing down sharply, and this decline will eventually shrink the pool of experienced people. The reserves are being reduced as well but not as much as the active forces. What does the difference in drawdown imply about the reserves' ability to recruit prior-service personnel?

THIS REPORT

To answer these questions and others, this report examines how the enlisted force of the Selected Reserve is changing and why. It provides an overview of recent trends in various personnel indicators: quality and experience of the force, its prior-service content, affiliation rates, skill match at entry, attrition and transfer rates, turbulence in units and jobs, and skill-qualification rates. The report focuses on changes from FY89 on, although it includes earlier data to provide historical context for the analysis. These data provide the long-term profile needed as a benchmark for future military personnel planning.

The data are drawn from two databases. These are matched longitudinal files from FY86–FY94 and active loss files for the same period. The latter data are matched with the reserve master files to identify which individuals leaving the active force join the reserves and when.

HOW ARE THE RESERVES DOING?

Our analysis of data through FY94 shows that:

- ODS/S has not adversely affected the reserves' ability to recruit or retain people.
- With respect to prior-service personnel, the reserves
  - — Have been successful at attracting them, and

— Have been doing a better job at matching the prior-service skill of recruits with their reserve assignment.

But

- Attrition among those who have joined without military experience appears to be on the increase, and
- In spite of better matching of prior-service skills and reserve duty assignments, skill qualification remains a problem, largely because of high turbulence.

CONCLUSIONS

Our analysis of recent personnel indicators suggests that the Selected Reserve Components have improved in a number of respects. They are fielding a senior, experienced, and high-quality enlisted force. They have been successful at increasing their prior-service content, although this increase results from a larger pool of assets as a result of the drawdown rather than an increased rate of joining. The reserves have markedly increased their job-match rates for new prior-service gains, and the attrition rates of these gains have also declined. Skill qualification remains stable, and turbulence shows modest improvement.

That said, there are some concerns. Attrition of those without prior service has increased. This increase may result from a conscious selection policy, as units choose to retain the more qualified prior-service people as the force shrinks. If not, this trend bears watching as retirements increase and the reserves take in more people without military experience.

Second, although turbulence at the job and unit level has remained the same or has even improved, it is still quite high, and it leads to high proportions of some components being unqualified. For example, about 30 percent of the Army Components are not qualified in their assigned skill. Low qualification rates lower readiness—and thus the ability to deploy—and increase training costs. Skill qualification remains a stubborn and systemic problem in the Reserve Components. To reduce turbulence within and across units will require substantial and wide-ranging reforms.

ACKNOWLEDGMENTS

We wish to thank Frank Rush and Wayne Spruell for their support of this study and the Defense Manpower Data Center for providing the data that form the basis of the analysis. The report benefited greatly from the helpful comments provided by our RAND colleagues, Ron Sortor and Harry Thie, who reviewed a draft of the final report, and Susan Hosek. We thank David Grissmer for several useful discussions during the course of the analysis, Dan Kohner and Richard Krimmer of Reserve Affairs for their helpful suggestions, and Jerry Sollinger for his recommendations on how to improve the readability and clarity of the report. We are grateful to Patricia Bedrosian for her careful and patient editing.

ACRONYMS

AC	Active Components
AFQT	Armed Forces Qualification Test
AFR	Air Force Reserve
AGR	Active Guard/Reserve
ANG	Air National Guard
ARNG	Army National Guard
AT	Annual Training
ETS	Enlisted Term of Service
FETY	Full-Time Equivalent Training Years
FTS	Full-Time Support
FY	Fiscal Year
IADT	Initial Active-Duty Training
MCR	Marine Corps Reserve
MOSQ	Military Occupational Specialty Qualification
NCO	Noncommissioned Officer
NPS	Nonprior Service
NR	Naval Reserve

ODS/S	Operation Desert Shield/Storm
OSD	Office of the Secretary of Defense
PS	Prior Service
RC	Reserve Components
RCCPDS	Reserve Component Common Personnel Data System
TAFMS	Total Active Federal Military Service
USAR	United States Army Reserve
USMC	United States Marine Corps
YOS	Years of Service

Chapter One

INTRODUCTION

The American military is undergoing a fundamental reshaping and restructuring brought about by the changing political and military global environment, changing domestic priorities, and tighter fiscal constraints. The "Total Force" Policy instituted in 1973 clearly specified that reserve forces would be "the initial and primary augmentation of active forces and military response would involve the integrated use of all forces available including active, reserve, civilian, and allied" (Brauner, Thie, and Brown, 1992, p. 1). During the 1980s, the Reserve Components grew rapidly as they were given more and more demanding missions. Before the beginning of the drawdown, the Selected Reserve forces were the largest and most experienced in recent history. Reserve Component endstrength peaked in FY89 at nearly 1.2 million Selected Reserve members. Operation Desert Storm provided an important reminder of the greater reliance on reserve forces. Over 245,000 reservists were mobilized. The October 1993 *Report on the Bottom-Up Review* by then Secretary of Defense Les Aspin recognized the Reserve Component forces as an integral part of our armed forces and "essential to the implementation of our defense strategy" (Aspin, 1993, p. 91).

Since then, as Figure 1.1 shows, reserve forces have been drawing down, although not to the extent that the active forces have. Reserve endstrength has declined by 14.7 percent from FY89 to FY94, and it is planned that the reserve will stabilize at just under 900,000 by the end of the drawdown. This will represent a 25 percent reduction from peak strength in FY89. The reserve drawdown is thus two-thirds complete.

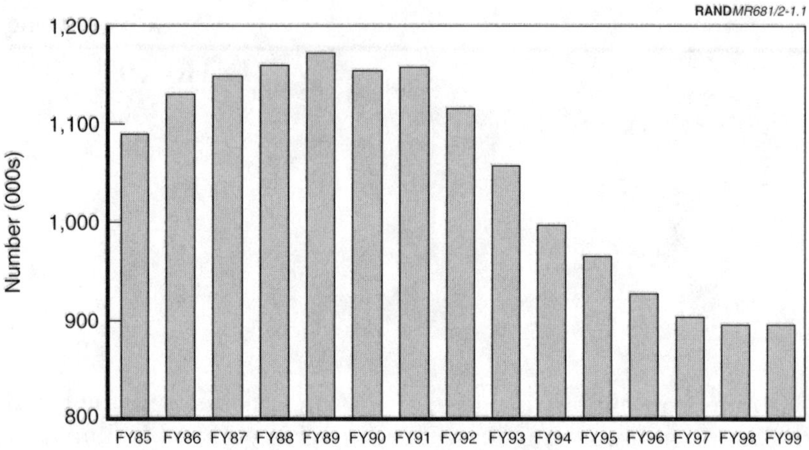

Figure 1.1—Selected Reserve Endstrengths, FY85–FY99

Despite the drawdown, fiscal constraints are placing a high priority on using reserve forces wherever they can meet deployment dates and readiness criteria. Currently, for example, the Air National Guard (ANG) provides all of the nation's air defense; the U.S. Army Reserve (USAR) provides all the chemical brigades and heavy helicopter units and about 70 percent of the medical assets of the Army; the Air Force Reserve (AFR) provides half the air crews for troop and supply movement to combat areas; 90 percent of cargo handling and shipping control is in the purview of the Naval Reserve (NR); and the Marine Corps Reserve (MCR) provides one of the four Marine divisions. It is expected that, by FY99, the Reserve Components will constitute 39 percent of the nation's defense force—up from 36 percent at the end of the Cold War.

In addition, the Reserve Components are expected to play an important role in responding to regional crises, as well as in peacekeeping, peace enforcement, and humanitarian assistance operations. Indeed, Reserve Component involvement in peacekeeping and humanitarian assistance operations, although still fairly limited, increased significantly over the past few years, as evidenced by the Army Sinai Initiative, reserve support of Somalia's Operations RESTORE HOPE and PROVIDE RELIEF, the 1993 Kiev medical mission, and numerous others (Aspin, 1993, pp. 41–54). Reservists have been an important part of the Bosnian and Somalian support sorties as well as the domestic emergency teams responding to floods, earthquakes, and hurricane-hit areas. The Assistant Secretary of Defense for Reserve Affairs, Deborah Lee, explicated the current strategy: "As we reduce the size of the Active component, we must use the National Guard and Reserve as a form of compensating leverage to reduce risks and contain defense costs in the post–Cold War era" (Department of Defense, 1994).

These roles and missions, combined with the downsizing of the active forces make the personnel sustentation of the reserve—that is, the ability of the reserve to meet the manpower and readiness requirements called for by our national military strategy—a critical issue. To a large extent, "the sustentation of the reserve depends crucially on the ability of the reserve to accomplish three objectives: recruit and retain prior-service (PS) personnel from the active forces; utilize their prior training effectively; and maintain low levels of attrition for all reserve personnel" (Grissmer and Kirby, 1994, p. 190). This report focuses on these three issues and tracks the recent performance of the Selected Reserve Components on these and related fronts.

Congressional concern about the lack of readiness of some units of the ARNG during ODS/S led to the passage of Title XI—the Army National Guard Combat Readiness Reform Act (U.S. House of Representatives, 1992). The legislation set PS content goals for the ARNG of 50 percent of enlisted members and 65 percent of officers; these goals were to be met by FY97. The definition of prior active service was two years of active-duty experience.

The drawdown of the active forces raises some serious concerns regarding the ability of the reserve to meet PS content goals and maintain the required levels of readiness (Grissmer et al., 1994a). The active force provides experienced personnel to the reserve forces; as the size of the active force declines, so would the flow of personnel with active-duty experience to the reserve forces. If these prior-service personnel are critical to the readiness of the Reserve Components and demand remained stable, reserve readiness would also decline.

Along with this potential disruption in the pipeline of prior-service personnel from the Active Component to the Reserve Component, especially for components that are already supply-constrained such as the Army Reserve Components, the report mentioned several other personnel problems facing the Reserve Components. These included high attrition and turnover among personnel—both those with and those without prior active service—and the large number of individuals in units who are not skill-qualified. In FY89, this level was between 20 and 30 percent for the Army components.

The earlier report also provided a snapshot of the Reserve Components as of the end of FY89 in terms of the mix of prior active service and nonprior-service personnel and linked PS content to various personnel readiness issues. It then projected how the PS content would change for each component under alternative active and reserve force sizes and mixes and estimated a potential reduction in PS content, particularly for the Army components. However, we also pointed out that the active drawdown offered a one-time bonanza for reserve recruiting and a unique opportunity for the components to increase their PS accessions and capitalize on the experience and training of these personnel.

More recent data allow us to examine whether and how the PS content of the Reserve Components has changed over time, and whether the reserves have been successful in attracting and keeping a larger share of the PS reserve pool. This report focuses on the Selected Reserve enlisted force and its changing profile, set against the context of the military drawdown and the end of the Cold War. It provides an overview of recent trends in various personnel indicators: quality and experience of the force; PS content, affiliation, and skill match at entry; component attrition and transfer rates; unit/job turbulence; and skill-qualification rates among different types of personnel. The main emphasis is on changes from FY89 on, although we provide earlier data in several cases to provide a longer history and context for the analysis. The data presented here provide a historical, comprehensive, and detailed profile of the Selected Reserve Components along a variety of readiness dimensions. Given the uncertain and changing environment, such data are needed to help provide a benchmark for military manpower planners and to act as a source of reference for future work in this area.

DATA

Our data comprise two sets of personnel files:

1. For each reservist from FY85 through FY94, we use quarterly snapshots taken from the Reserve Component Common Personnel Data System (RCCPDS) master files. These were matched by Social Security Number to provide a longitudinal history of each reservist. The data analysis is based on a 10 percent random sample (for the inventory analysis) and a 30 percent random sample (for the analysis of gain cohorts).
2. For the accession analysis, we use active loss files from FY86 through FY94 matched to the reserve master files to see if and when individuals leaving the active force join the Selected Reserve.

DEFINITION OF PS AND NPS

The Congressional goals defined prior service as 24 months of active duty. Presumably this was set to correspond to the shortest active-duty term available to enlistees. However, as we discussed in our earlier report (Grissmer et al., 1994a), the Congressional language failed to specify precisely what constituted "active duty." Reservists are given credit for active duty when attending two weeks of annual training (AT), initial active-duty training (IADT), or certain military schools for training. By attending IADT, annual training over a number of years, and other associated training schools, a reservist with no prior active service could accumulate sufficient active-duty days over a period of years to meet the Congressional definition. Presumably the intent of Congress was not to include such individuals in the PS definition. Therefore, our definition attempts to count only continuous active service as a member of the Active Component by excluding annual training days.

More precisely, we estimate the months of active duty by adjusting the data field—total active federal military service (TAFMS)—obtained from the RCCPDS records that form our main source of data. TAFMS measures the months of active-duty military service but also includes time spent in annual training, IADT, and other formal school training in active-duty schools. Although we do not have the data that would allow us to fully adjust TAFMS, we do adjust for the increment due to annual training days. This is done by subtracting annual training days that accrue to TAFMS throughout a reserve career. Using this corrected TAFMS measure, we defined as PS those with TAFMS ≥ 24 months. Our earlier analysis of FY88–FY89 data showed that the ARNG and MCR did not increment TAFMS for annual training days. For these components, we used TAFMS directly rather than the adjusted TAFMS.

We should clarify one further definitional issue. Accessions to the Reserve Components consist of both those with and those without prior active service. However, it is occasionally important for some types of analyses to further distinguish the latter category into those with and without prior *reserve* service. The latter are truly nonprior-service personnel and the term NPS in common usage is reserved for them. We follow this usage. Those who enter the Selected Reserve who have had some prior reserve experience are referred to as "prior reserve service" gains.

ORGANIZATION OF THE REPORT

The second chapter presents a profile of the inventory of each Reserve Component at selected points in time and describes how these have changed over time. Because the changes in the inventory are driven by the gains to and losses from the inventory, we also examine the profile of gains from all sources: PS, NPS and those with prior reserve experience, their quality, and experience levels.

Chapter Three focuses on one particular type of gain: new prior-service entrants into the Selected Reserve Components. It uses active-duty loss cohorts to examine accession rates, the rate of skill match at entry—a crucial indicator in determining the extent of retraining required—and how long these individuals stay. Trends in the reserve joining and leaving rates of new active-duty losses are important in seeing how successful the Reserve Components have been in recruiting from the much larger pool of prior active-duty personnel created by the active drawdown and in retaining such entrants. Note that the definition of PS is much broader in Chapter Two than in Chapter Three. Chapter Three focuses on gains who entered the Selected Reserve after leaving the active force; i.e., they were *new* prior-service entrants. However, in setting PS content goals, Congress defined PS as those reservists with two or more years of active-duty experience. Therefore, Chapter Two (as well as later chapters) adopts the broader PS definition and includes as PS gains those with two or more years of active experience, regardless of whether their last military experience was with the reserve or with the active force—in other words, gains who would count toward meeting the Congressionally mandated PS content goal. Despite the seeming contradiction, both analyses are needed to round out the complete picture of how the enlisted force is changing and why—one examines the ability and success of the Reserve Components in attracting individuals newly leaving the active force; the other examines whether the reserves are making progress in terms of meeting or exceeding Congressional goals.

Chapter Four examines attrition from both the inventory and the gain cohorts, disaggregated by type of personnel and type of attrition—temporary and permanent. All these chapters focus on personnel indicators at the component level. However, aggregate statistics fail to paint a complete picture of unit readiness.

Chapter Five, therefore, describes unit and job turbulence in the Reserve Components—two other indicators that have an immediate effect on unit readiness.

Conclusions are presented in Chapter Six.

Chapter Two

CHANGING PROFILE OF THE RESERVE COMPONENTS, FY85–FY94

This chapter examines the changing profile of the reserve inventory as well as new reserve gains in terms of experience, type of personnel, and quality. The data on which our analysis is based consist of a longitudinal reserve master file of Selected reservists.

PROFILE OF THE INVENTORY

Full-Time Support Personnel

The Selected Reserve consists primarily of part-time reservists who generally drill once a month and attend active-duty training for two weeks in the year. However, a small proportion of reserve personnel serve full-time. Although our primary focus is the part-time enlisted force, we start by examining the level of full-time support (FTS) in the Reserve Components. FTS is regarded as critical to Reserve Component unit readiness; the 1993 *Report of the Reserve Forces Policy Board* (Department of Defense, 1994) describes the number of FTS personnel as a "force multiplier" that enables drilling reservists to take maximum advantage of the limited training time available and relieves commanders of onerous administrative duties. In addition, such personnel often provide "continuity and stability vital to the success of Reserve units" (p. 50). FTS personnel consist of Active Guard/Reserve (AGR) personnel, military technicians and Air Reserve technicians, Active Component personnel who directly support reserve units, and civil service personnel.

Figure 2.1 shows the proportion of full-time personnel in the different Reserve Components and how this has changed over time. There are substantial differences in the level of FTS among the Reserve Components: FTS personnel account for almost 30 percent of the ANG enlisted force, whereas USAR and MCR have substantially lower percentages of FTS personnel, approximately 5 percent (see also Brauner and Gotz, 1991).[1] About 10 percent of the ARNG enlisted force and 15 percent of NR and AFR are FTS personnel. Over time, the proportion of the force filled by FTS personnel has increased modestly in every component. The *Bottom-Up Review* (Aspin, 1993) specifically mentions that the USAR was slated to have a higher percentage of FTS personnel as part of a set of initiatives aimed at improving the readiness and availability of the Reserve Components, so it is likely that the percentages shown here for the USAR may be even higher in the future.

Most of the FTS personnel—90 percent or over, depending on component—tend to be PS personnel. We focus our report on part-

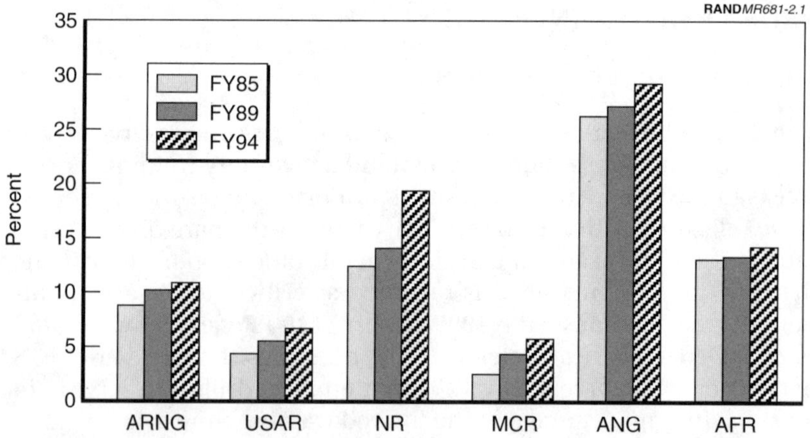

Figure 2.1—Percentage of Full-Time Enlisted Personnel in the Reserve Components, FY85, FY89, and FY94

---

[1]The Marine Corps Reserve has a deliberate policy of hiring predominantly NPS individuals and this is in keeping with its mission, which is primarily combat. Hence the low PS content is not seen as a matter of concern.

timers for several reasons: Part-time Selected reservists constitute between 75 and 95 percent of the enlisted force; they are likely to be the most vulnerable to changes in experience mix resulting from the active force drawdown; and they tend to face the most problems in terms of attrition, unit/job turbulence, and skill mismatch.

PS Content of Reserve Inventory, FY85–FY94

The proportions of prior active service personnel—defined as those with two or more years of active-duty experience as measured by the corrected TAFMS measure[2]—in the part-time enlisted force are presented in Figures 2.2–2.4 for the six Reserve Components and for the FY85, FY89, and FY94 inventories. The AFR has the highest percentage of PS enlisted among all the components—71 percent in FY94—whereas the MCR has the lowest—a little over 15 percent. Over half of the FY94 NR and ANG enlisted personnel have prior active service, whereas about 35 percent of the two Army components are PS.

RANDMR681-2.2

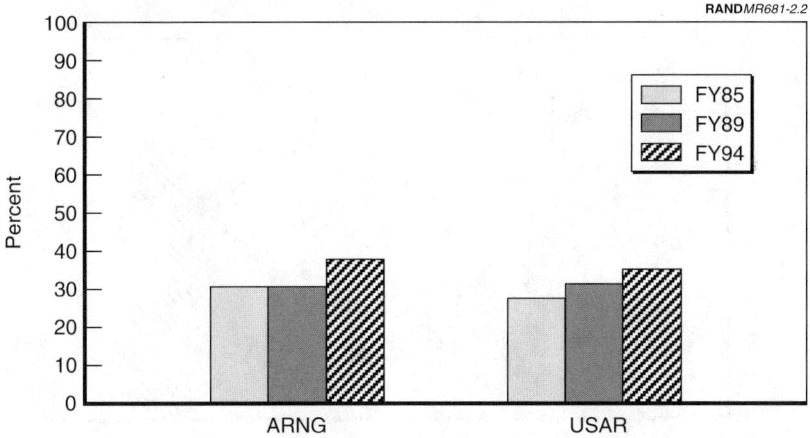

Figure 2.2—Percentage of Part-Time Enlisted Personnel with Prior Active Service in the ARNG and USAR, FY85, FY89, and FY94

---

[2]See Chapter One for a description of the corrected TAFMS measure.

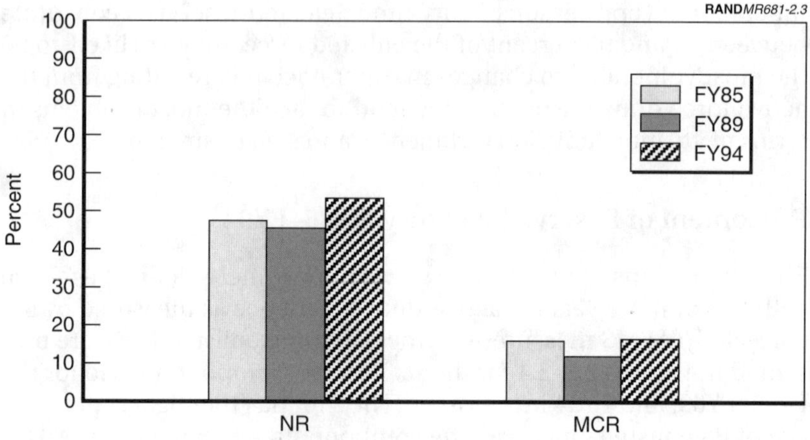

Figure 2.3—Percentage of Part-Time Enlisted Personnel with Prior Active Service in the NR and MCR, FY85, FY89, and FY94

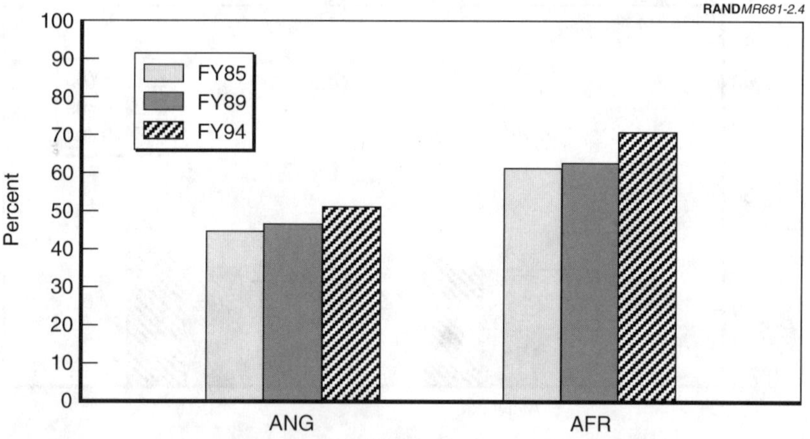

Figure 2.4—Percentage of Part-Time Enlisted Personnel with Prior Active Service in the ANG and AFR, FY85, FY89, and FY94

What is interesting is that almost all the Reserve Components have increased their PS content over time, in most cases by about 5 percentage points between FY89 and FY94. This suggests that the

Reserve Components have indeed been successful in attracting and retaining increased numbers of PS personnel over this time period; the evidence we present below in this chapter and in Chapter Three shows that this is indeed the case.

However, the numbers also point to the difficulty of meeting the Title XI goals of 50 percent PS content for the enlisted force for the ARNG. In FY94, 11 percent of ARNG personnel were FTS, 90 percent of them PS. About 37 percent of the part-timers meet the Congressional definition for PS.

This means that for the FY94 inventory as a whole, counting both part-time and full-time personnel, the PS content of the ARNG was 43 percent. As retirements increase from the Selected Reserve, and as the pool of PS personnel from which the Reserve Components can recruit decreases in size, it may become harder in the future to maintain or increase these PS levels, particularly if the size of the Selected Reserve remains fairly stable.

Minorities in the Reserve Components

Data on the racial/ethnic makeup of the Reserve Components are presented to provide a more complete profile of the enlisted force and to help answer frequently raised questions regarding the representativeness of the Reserve Components. Overall, the Reserve Components have a higher representation of blacks and Hispanics[3] than in the overall population,[4] but there are sizable differences in black and Hispanic representation across the Reserve Components, as shown in Figure 2.5. The USAR has the highest proportion of blacks and Hispanics among all the components: 32 percent in FY89 and 35 percent in FY94. Almost the entire increase was accounted for by an increase in the number of Hispanics. Blacks and Hispanics account for about 25 percent of the ARNG, MCR, and AFR; the proportions are somewhat smaller for the NR and ANG. In almost every component, the proportion of the force that is Hispanic rose from

[3]The personnel records classify reservists as white, black, Hispanic, American Indian/Alaskan, Asian/Pacific Islander, other, and unknown.

[4]To set this in context, in 1990, 71.8 percent of the total U.S. population was white, whereas blacks and Hispanics constituted 11.7 and 9.0 percent, respectively.

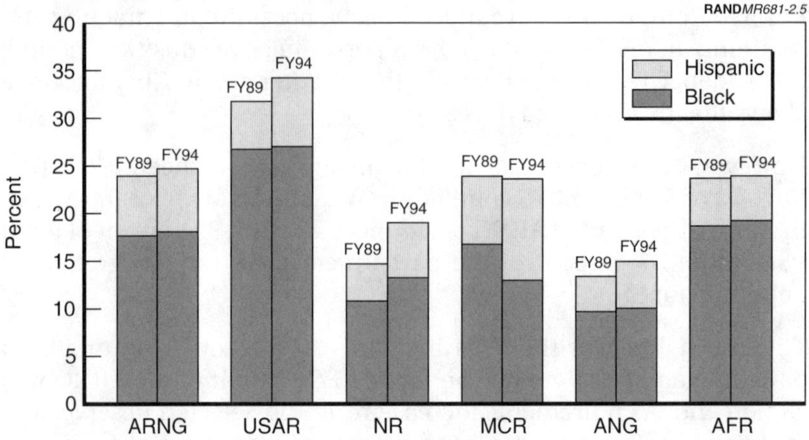

Figure 2.5—Percentage of Blacks and Hispanics in the Reserve Components, FY89 and FY94

FY89 to FY94, suggesting that the components have been successful in attracting and retaining Hispanic recruits.

Women in the Reserve Components

Overall, women constitute 13 percent of the Selected Reserve strength (compared to 11.6 percent for the Active Components). Figure 2.6 shows the percentage of women in each of the Reserve Components, ranging from a high of 22 percent in the USAR and AFR to a low of 7.5 percent in the ARNG and 3 percent in the MCR. The low proportions in the ARNG and MCR can be explained by the preponderance of combat specialties in these two components and the service combat exclusion policies that define those combat-related career fields to which women cannot be assigned. However, the opening of combat aviation units to women made several additional positions available to them in the ARNG (as well as in other components) and the MCR expanded several career fields to women during FY93–FY94 (embarkation officer, ground nuclear weapons assembly technician, etc.), so the proportions shown here may rise slightly in the future.

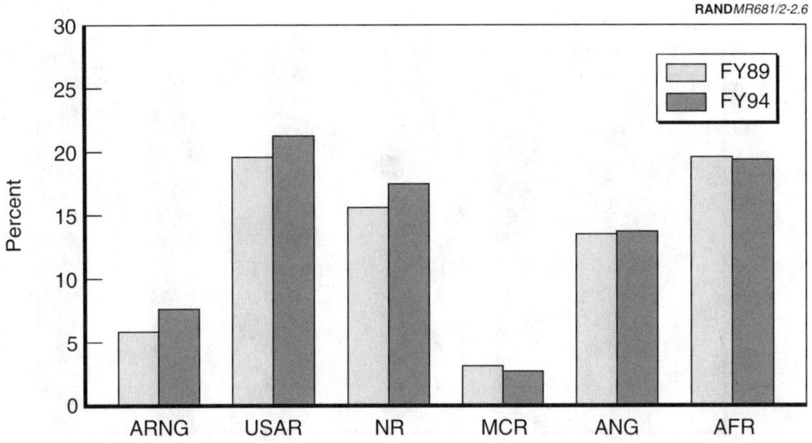

Figure 2.6—Percentage of Women in the Reserve Components, FY89 and FY94

Quality of the Enlisted Force

Education and aptitude are the two main measures of the potential trainability, performance, and likely retention behavior of enlisted recruits. Research on early enlisted active and reserve attrition during training and before completing terms of service shows that higher education and aptitude are linked to lower attrition as well as to higher promotion rates among enlisted personnel.[5]

The quality of the enlisted force has improved steadily over time, as shown in the next two graphs. The percentage of high school graduates in the enlisted force, shown in Figure 2.7, is 87 percent in the ARNG and well over 95 percent in the remaining Reserve Components. As can be seen, this number increased by 3–5 percentage points between FY89 and FY94. Many of the remaining enlisted reservists have a General Equivalency Diploma.

[5]See Grissmer et al. (1994a) for a complete list of references to this literature.

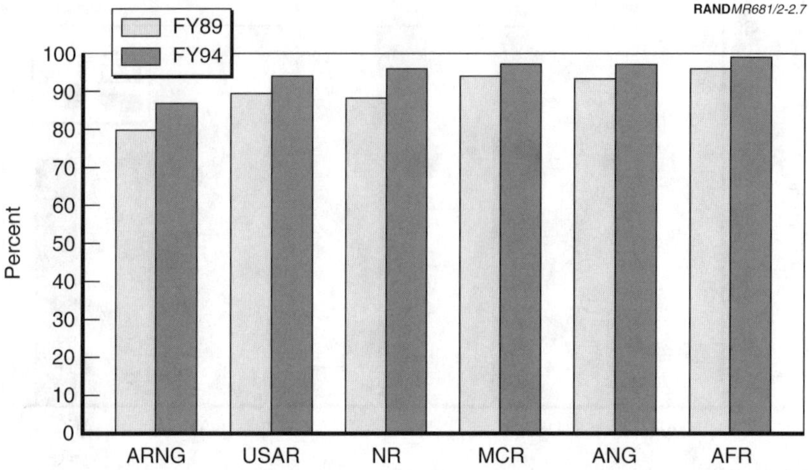

Figure 2.7—Percentage of High School Graduates in the Reserve Components, FY89 and FY94

In terms of aptitude, we find that the proportion of the enlisted force[6] that scored in the upper half of the aptitude distribution—that is, those scoring in the 50th percentile or higher, generally referred to as Category I–IIIA—is quite high and has increased modestly over time (Figure 2.8). For example, in FY89, the percentage of the enlisted force that was Category I–IIIA ranged from 60 percent in the ARNG, and 68 percent in the USAR to 70 percent and higher in the remaining four components. This proportion increased by 1 to 3 percentage points for all components from FY89–FY94; the exception was the MCR, where the gain was somewhat larger, about 6 percentage points.

[6]Because we are looking at the aptitude of all personnel in the inventory—not all of whom took or were required to take the Armed Forces Qualification Test (AFQT), on which these categories are based—we are missing data for between 5 and 20 percent of cases. However, for the Naval Reserve, almost 45 percent of all personnel were missing AFQT scores. The percentages shown here are calculated using available data only. There are no clear patterns over time with respect to the proportion of cases missing data.

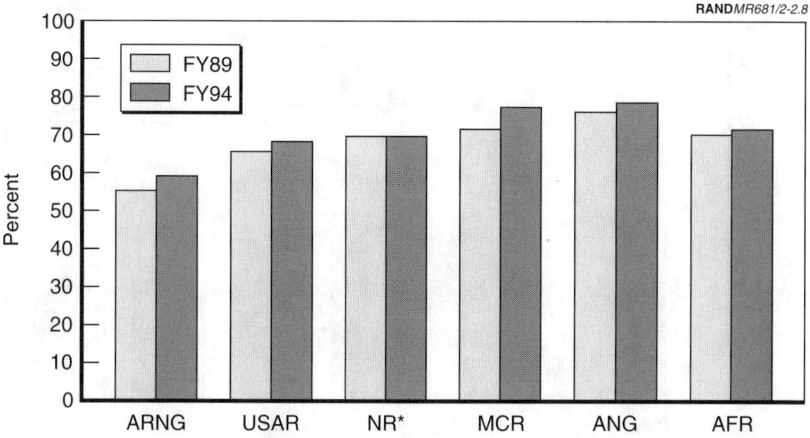

*Between 35-45 percent were missing data.

Figure 2.8—Percentage Rated Category I–IIIA in the Reserve Components, FY89 and FY94

Military Experience

As Figure 2.9 shows, the Reserve Components appear to have very experienced personnel.[7] In FY89, only 18 percent of the enlisted force had no prior active military experience. One-third of the force had 10 or more years of service; 19 percent had 15 or more years of service. Over time, the force is aging and becoming more experienced, which has some implications both for costs now and for recruiting a few years down the road. By FY94, only 13 percent of the

[7]Our earlier report (Grissmer et al., 1994a) developed a new measure of military experience, called full-time equivalent training years (FETY), which focused specifically on the amount of time available for practicing military skills and on the different kinds of personnel in the reserve for whom this available time differs. We argued that this measure—despite shortcomings that we pointed out in the report—allowed more accurate comparisons between PS and NPS personnel, in terms of overall potential difference in experience, than the more traditional years of service (YOS) measure, which is merely the sum of active and reserve years of service. Here, because our goal is not so much to compare the equivalent experience of different types of personnel but to see how the overall experience of the enlisted force has changed over time, we use the traditional YOS measure.

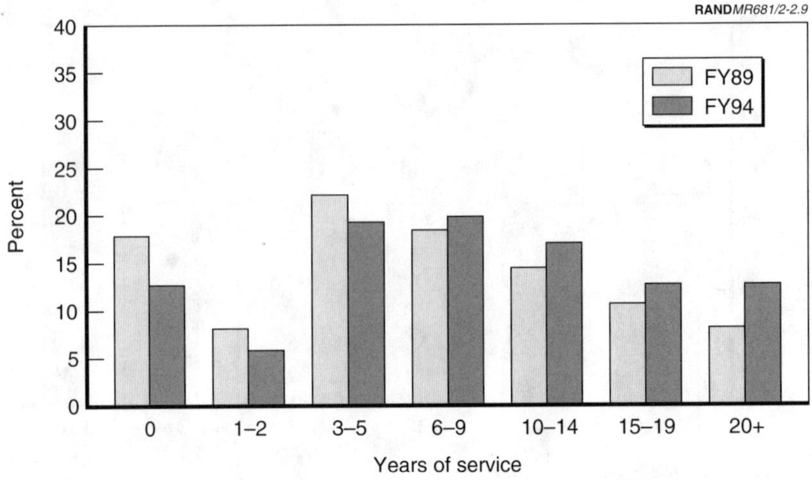

Figure 2.9—Percentage of Personnel by Years of Service, FY89 and FY94

force was NPS, as the components reduced NPS accessions in favor of taking in more prior-service personnel. Over 40 percent of the FY94 part-time enlisted personnel had 10 or more years of service, whereas a quarter of the enlisted force had 15 or more years of service. This is a very senior force and appears to be becoming even more so. However, the Selected Reserve drawdown, the transition benefits implemented by DoD[8] that are aimed primarily (although not exclusively) at those with 15 or more years of service particularly in units that are being downsized and deactivated due to the drawdown, and the eventual retirement of large numbers of very senior people in the next several years will likely lead to a significant change in the experience profile of the Reserve Components. The potential effect of this change on recruiting and training costs and readiness of the Reserve Components needs to be carefully considered.

We had earlier mentioned the importance of PS personnel to the Selected Reserve. Although those without prior active service can

[8]These include (among others) special separation pay for those with 20 or more years of service, early qualification for retired pay for those with 15–20 years of service who are involuntarily separated, and separation pay for those with 6–15 years of service who are involuntarily discharged from the reserve.

bring civilian skills to reserve jobs, PS personnel bring at least three experience-related advantages to reserve service:

- Proficiency and experience in a specific skill;
- Generic military knowledge, experience, and culture not associated with a specific occupational skill; and
- Completion of a prescreening process that may lower the costs of successfully filling reserve jobs.

It is important to track the level of experience that PS personnel bring with them to the reserve and how this has changed over time. Figure 2.10 profiles the active military experience of PS personnel in terms of years of active service for the FY89 and FY94 inventories. About 57 percent of PS personnel in FY89 had from 2–4 years of active service (they were presumably first-termers in the Active Component); a quarter had from 4–6 years of active service, and another 14 percent had from 6–10 years of service. Less than 5 percent had 10 or more years of active service. In FY94, however, the profile is a little different. The force as a whole has more experience:

RANDMR681/2-2.10

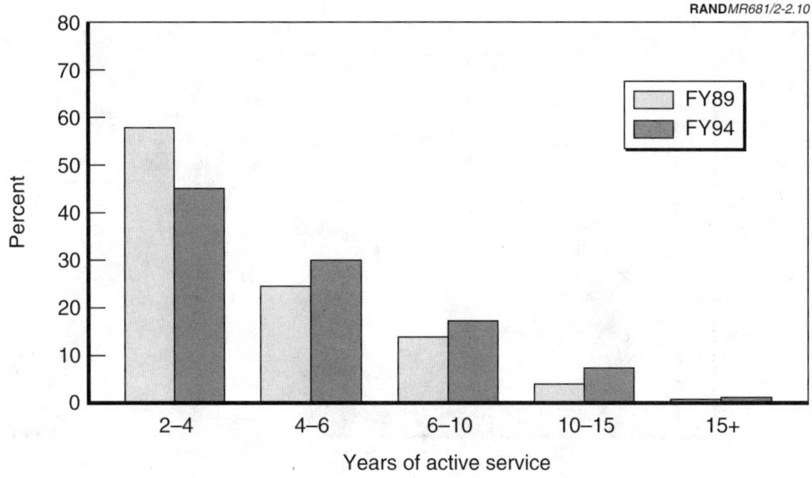

Figure 2.10—Percentage of Enlisted Personnel with Prior Active Service by Years of Active Service, FY89 and FY94

Fewer than half have less than 4 years of active service (a drop of 12 percentage points), 30 percent have from 4–6 years of service, and close to 8 percent have 10 or more years of service. Part of this increase in experience may be the result of Operation Desert Storm when 250,000 reservists were recalled to active duty. However, it is also likely that the Reserve Components have been quite successful in attracting more experienced PS personnel in the wake of the active drawdown—an issue that is addressed in some detail below.

Although Figure 2.10 presented the overall profile of the enlisted force in terms of active-duty experience, we felt it might be instructive to see whether the active-duty experience profile differs across the six Reserve Components (Figures 2.11–2.16). In FY94, a little under half of the ARNG PS reservists have from 2–4 years of active-duty experience; for the USAR, this proportion was 60 percent. The proportion of those with 2–4 years of service in the NR was about 40 percent and the remaining components have much smaller proportions—from 15–30 percent. The two Air Reserve Components along with the NR have the most experienced PS members: Over a quarter to a third of their PS members have 6 or more years of active service.

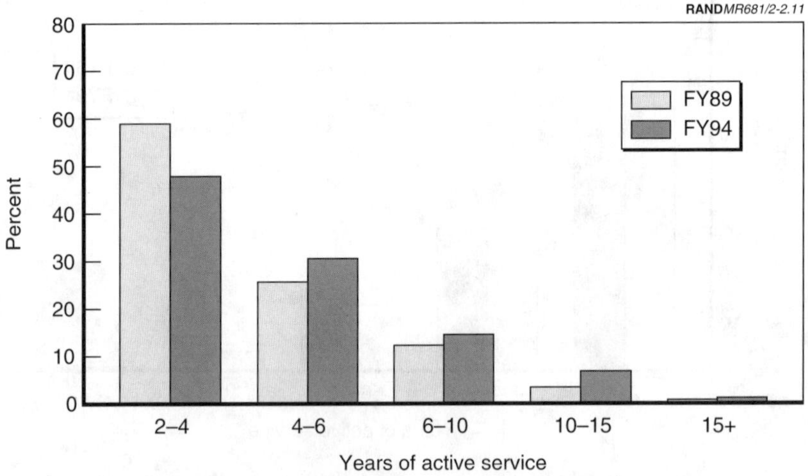

Figure 2.11—Percentage of Personnel with Prior Active Service in the ARNG by Years of Active Service, FY89 and FY94

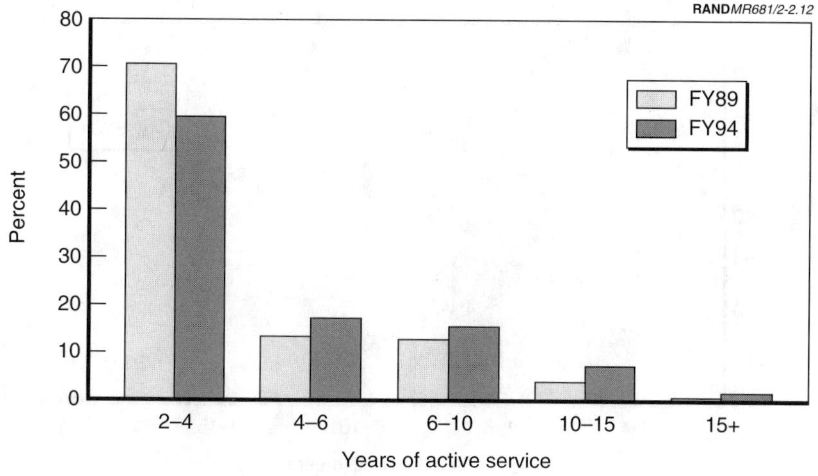

Figure 2.12—Percentage of Personnel with Prior Active Service in the USAR by Years of Active Service, FY89 and FY94

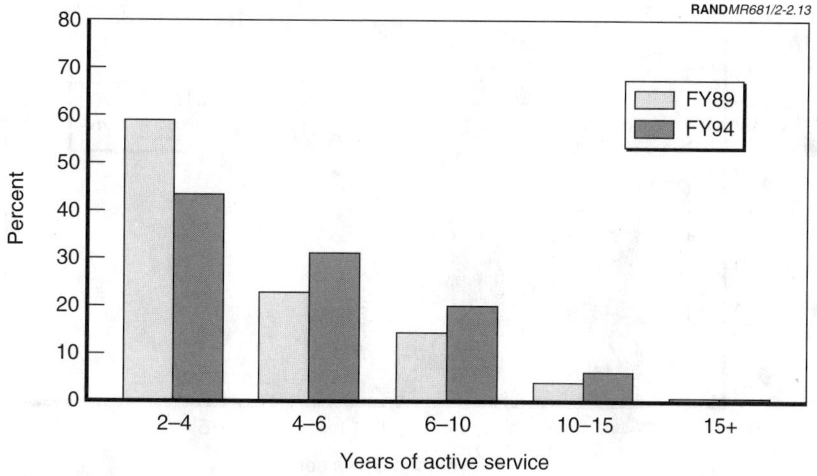

Figure 2.13—Percentage of Personnel with Prior Active Service in the NR by Years of Active Service, FY89 and FY94

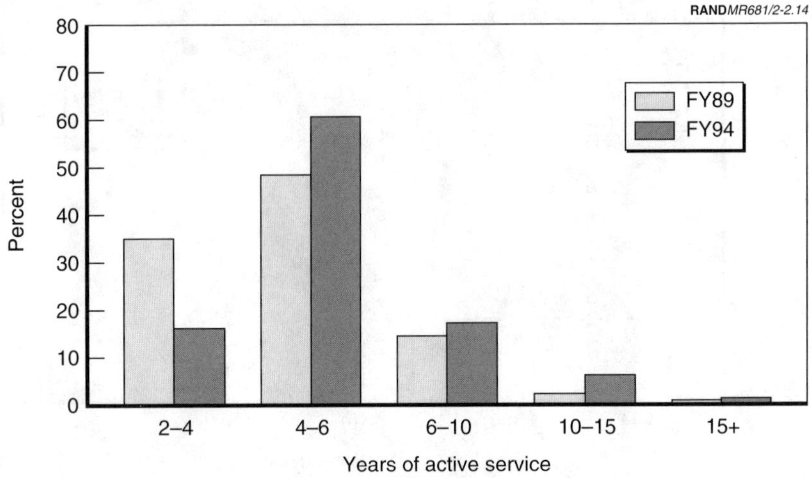

Figure 2.14—Percentage of Personnel with Prior Active Service in the MCR by Years of Active Service, FY89 and FY94

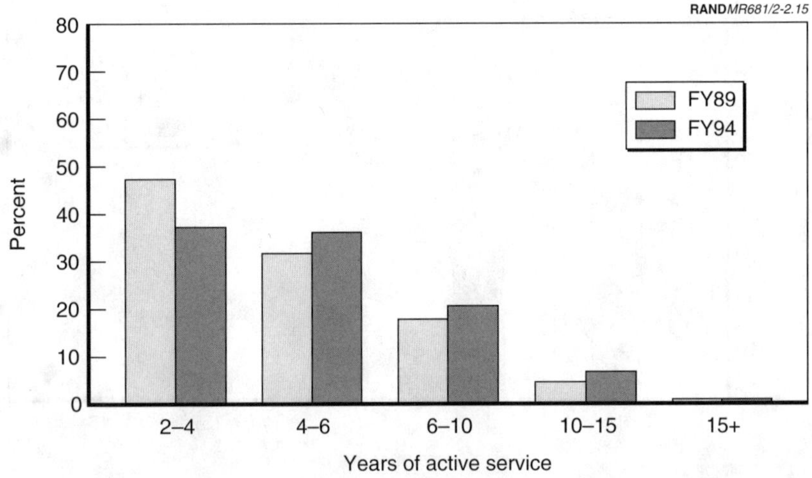

Figure 2.15—Percentage of Personnel with Prior Active Service in the ANG by Years of Active Service, FY89 and FY94

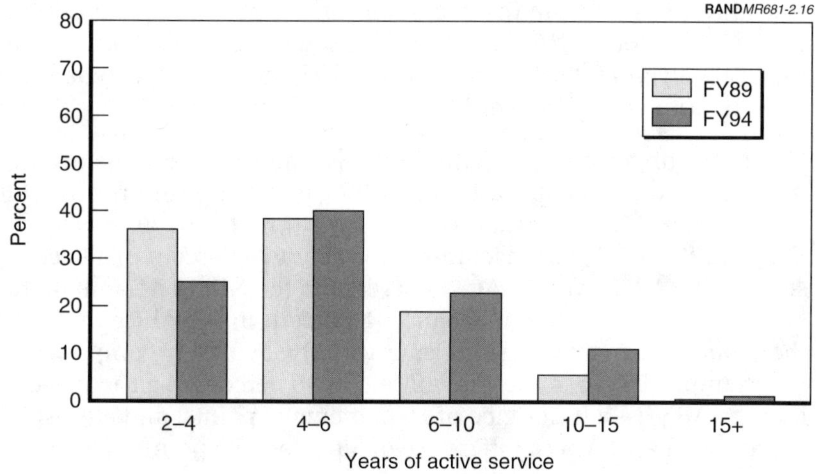

Figure 2.16—Percentage of Personnel with Prior Active Service in the AFR by Years of Active Service, FY89 and FY94

PROFILE OF GAINS, FY89–FY94

We have seen that the inventory profile of the Reserve Components has changed in significant ways over time. Clearly these changes are driven by the type and quality of accessions and the type and rate of losses from the Reserve Components. Attrition rates are considered in Chapters 3 and 4. This chapter briefly profiles gains into the Selected Reserve.[9] Because the major emphasis in this report is on recent changes in personnel trends and the effect of the drawdown and Operation Desert Storm, the analysis shown here focuses on gains between FY89 and FY94. These data are for part-timers only.

Reserve Gains by Type of Personnel

We can distinguish three types of accessions, based on years of total military service and years of active service, in particular: (a) NPS (those with no prior military experience); (b) prior reserve service

[9]As mentioned above, this analysis is based on a 30 percent sample, rather than a 10 percent sample, to obtain adequate sample sizes.

(those returning to the reserve, after having previously served in a Reserve Component, but with less than two years of prior active-duty experience); and (c) prior active service (PS—those with two or more years of prior active service).[10]

However, for purposes of Title XI goals, the PS accessions are the most important. Figure 2.17 show PS gains as a proportion of all gains, for each Reserve Component over time for FY89, FY93, and FY94. In FY89, PS gains accounted for about 30 percent of all accessions in the ARNG and USAR, 25 percent in the NR, 19 percent in the MCR, 47 percent in the ANG, and 64 percent in the AFR. By FY93, these numbers increased significantly for the two Army components. For example, PS personnel accounted for 40 percent of all accessions into the ARNG—a difference of 10 percentage points, and almost 35 percent in the USAR—a difference of 5 percentage points. However,

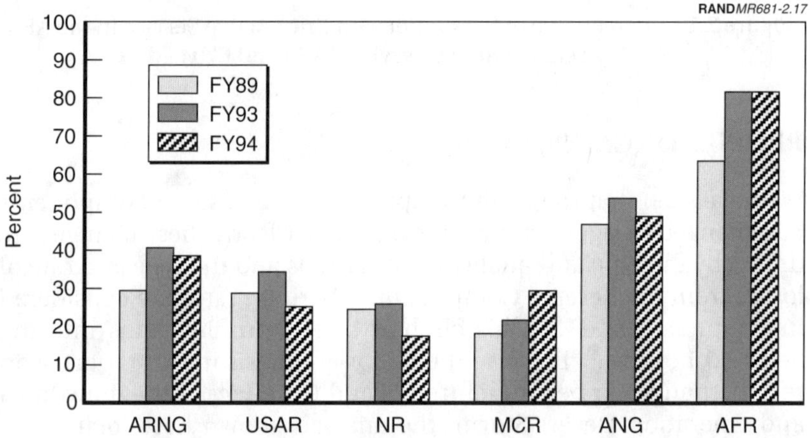

Figure 2.17—Percentage of Prior Active Service Gains into the Selected Reserve, FY89, FY93, and FY94

---

[10]As we mentioned in Chapter One, the categories are not as distinct as one would wish. The number in the prior active service (PS) category is an overestimate of those actually being gained from the Active Component—the subject of Chapter Three. The personnel described as PS here were originally gained from the AC, but they may have served in the reserve as well, and may be returning to the reserve after a separation. Thus, they belong both in the PS and prior reserve service categories. However, because they fulfill the Congressional definition of PS, they are classified as PS.

the FY94 numbers show a marked decline in the case of the USAR. The Air Reserve Components also show substantial increases from FY89 to FY94: The ANG PS gains form 54 percent of all part-time accessions and almost 82 percent of AFR gains have prior active service. This suggests that the Reserve Components have been quite successful in attracting PS accessions. However, we must caution that, as we mentioned in a footnote above, not all of these gains come directly from the AC; some have previously served in the reserve.

The decline in the proportion of PS gains evident in FY94 in most components needs further investigation. If these data are correct and the downward trend continues, it might suggest that the bonanza period of recruiting from the larger PS pool created by the drawdown might be coming to a close, making high levels of PS content harder to maintain in the future.

Prior Military Experience of Gains

Prior Active Service Gains: The next three figures (Figures 2.18–2.20) profile the active-duty experience level of PS accessions into each of the Selected Reserve Components for FY89 and FY94. Overall, the pattern is as we expected and offers good news about recruiting for the reserve. The reserves are attracting somewhat more experienced personnel in FY94 than in FY89 and appear to have been quite successful in taking advantage of the large pool of prior-service personnel created by the active drawdown.

For example, the proportion of those with 2–4 years of active service in FY89 compared to FY94 dropped from 54 to 35 percent in the ARNG, from 72 to 52 percent in the USAR, from 55 to 39 percent in the NR, from 28 to 8 percent in the MCR, from 46 to 25 percent in the ANG, and from 42 to 19 percent in the AFR, whereas the proportion of those with more than 4 years of service rose concomitantly. Indeed, in some components, the proportion of accessions with 10 or more years of active service has increased fourfold from FY89 to FY94.

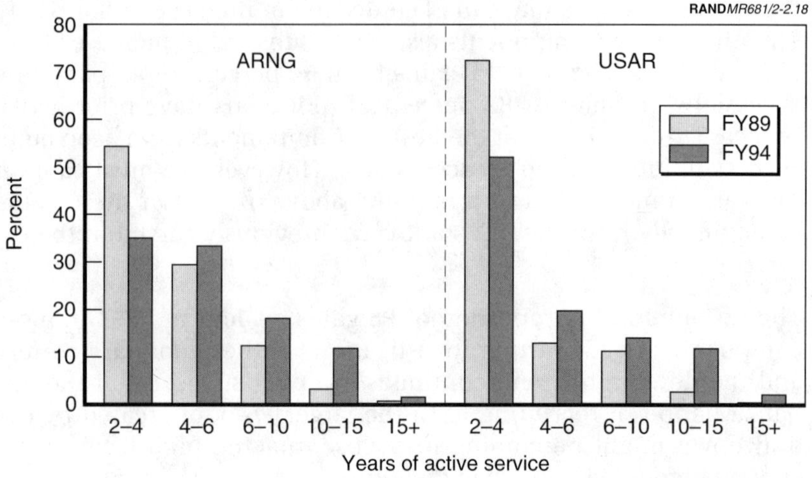

Figure 2.18—Percentage of Prior-Service Gains into the ARNG and USAR Selected Reserve with Prior Active Service Experience, FY89 and FY94

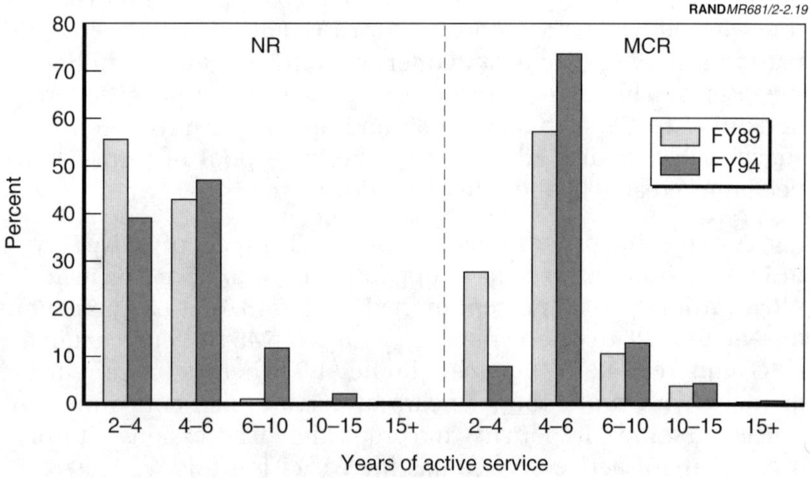

Figure 2.19—Percentage of Prior-Service Gains into the NR and MCR Selected Reserve with Prior Active Service Experience, FY89 and FY94

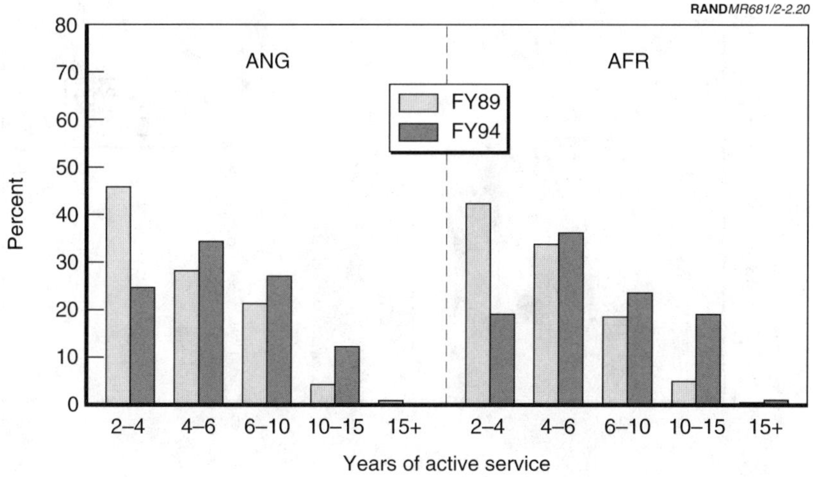

Figure 2.20—Percentage of Prior-Service Gains into the ANG and AFR Selected Reserve with Prior Active Service Experience, FY89 and FY94

Prior Reserve Service Gains: We find the same shift toward recruiting more experienced personnel among the prior reserve service gains as well. Although we do not show the breakdown for each component, the patterns are quite similar to the one shown in Figure 2.21, which compares the experience profile of the FY89 prior reserve service gains with that of the FY94 gains. As the graph makes clear, the reserves are attracting back larger proportions of more experienced personnel in FY94 than they were in FY89. For example, those with 10 or more years of service constituted 9 percent of all prior reserve service gains in FY89; by FY94, this proportion has almost doubled, to 17 percent. Again, although this means that we are fielding an extremely experienced force in FY94, there are implications for personnel costs and recruiting further down the road, as these reservists begin to approach retirement.

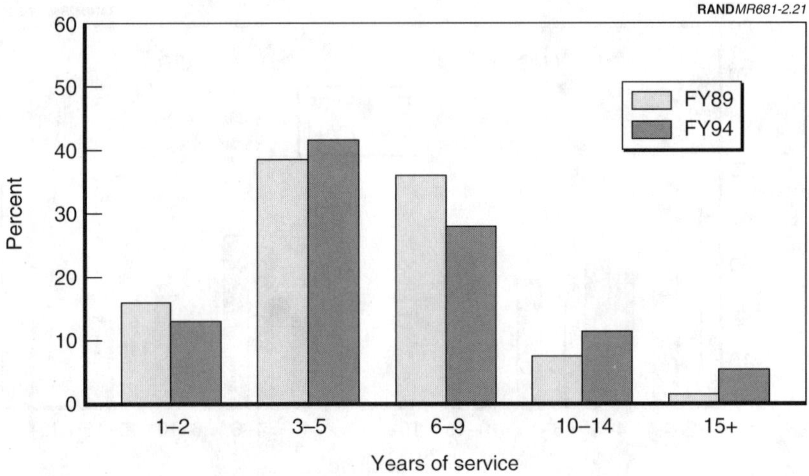

Figure 2.21—Percentage of Prior-Service Gains into the Selected Reserve with Prior Reserve Experience , FY89 and FY94

Quality of NPS Enlisted Gains

Nonprior-service enlisted gains constitute from 20 to 70 percent of all gains, depending on component. The Reserve Components experienced no decline in the quality of the nonprior-service enlisted gains from FY89 to FY94, and indeed, saw some modest gains as shown in Figures 2.22 and 2.23. The percentage of high school graduates increased or remained constant in every component; by FY94, well over 90 percent of recruits were high school graduates. The remainder were those with GED certificates.

Similarly, we see an increase in recruits scoring at the 50th percentile and above on the AFQT from FY89 to FY94 for almost every component. Unfortunately, the large amount of missing data made it impossible to calculate comparable numbers for the NR. The proportions of recruits who are Category I–IIIA ranged from 55 percent in the ARNG to close to 80 percent in the MCR and the two Air Reserve Components in FY94. This reflects an increase of from 1–10 percentage points over the FY89 numbers.

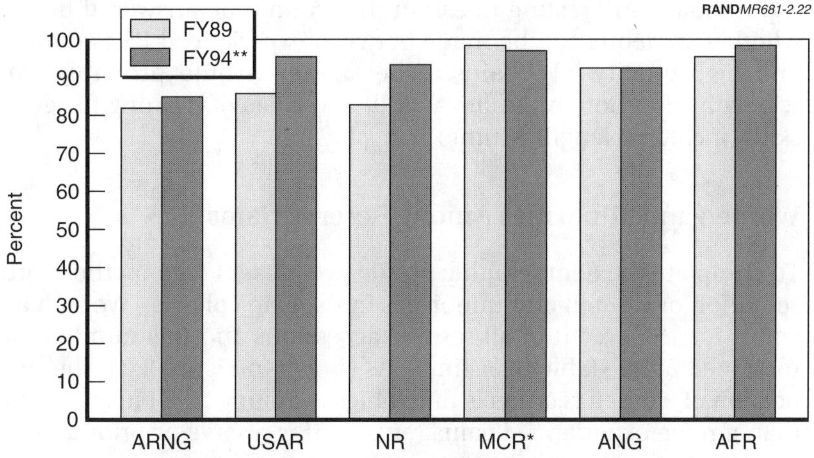

*About 16 percent of MCR recruits were missing data on education.
**Most of the remaining are alternative certification graduates.

Figure 2.22—Percentage of High School Graduates Among Nonprior-Service Enlisted Gains, FY89 and FY94

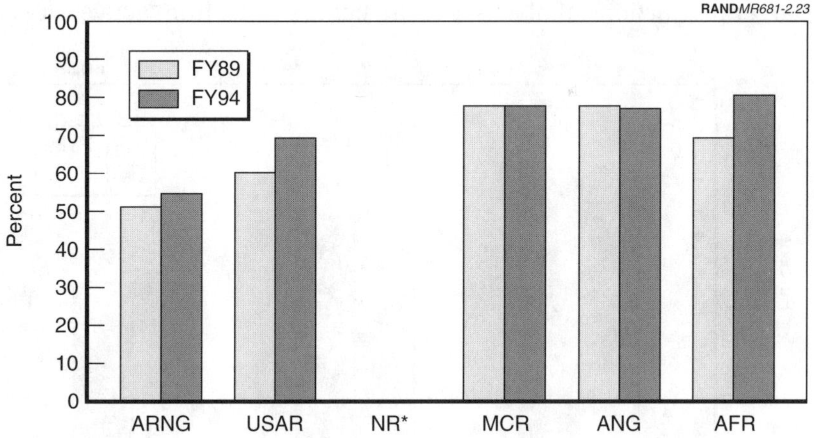

*A very high proportion of cases were missing data on AFQT scores.

Figure 2.23—Percentage Rated Category I–IIIA Among Nonprior-Service Enlisted Gains, FY89 and FY94

A potentially interesting question that cannot be answered here is whether tradeoffs can be made between experienced PS personnel and high-quality NPS gains. The answers would probably vary widely by component, military skill, and costs of training for given skills (including length of time).

Women and Minorities Among Reserve Gains

To complete the demographic profile, we present data on the representation of women and minorities in the gain cohorts. Women account for 15 percent of all reserve accessions and this number has remained fairly stable over time. As shown in Figure 2.24, the proportion of women recruits is much higher among NPS enlisted gains than among experienced gains (either prior reserve or prior active). There has been a small increase in the proportion of women recruits among both nonprior and prior reserve gains.

Overall, blacks and Hispanics account for 24 percent of all gains between FY89 and FY94. There are differences in trends depending on whether one looks at NPS, prior reserve service, or PS recruits (Figure 2.25). The proportion of NPS blacks being recruited has declined from 21 to 16 percent from FY89 to FY94 but this is offset by the larger proportions of blacks who are being gained from active service

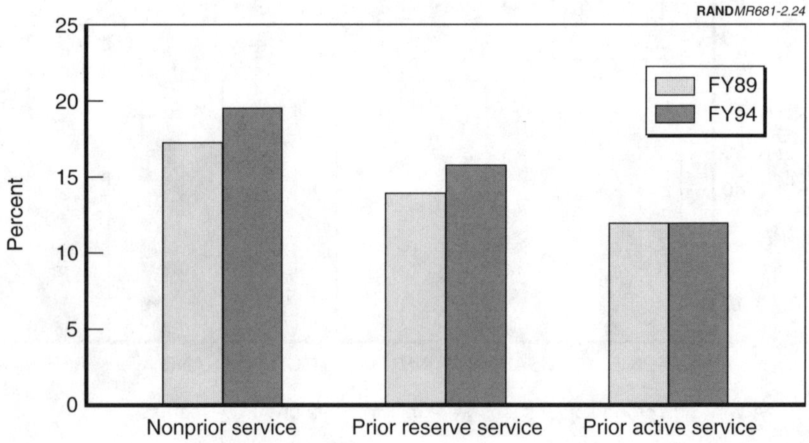

Figure 2.24—Percentage of Women Among Enlisted Gains, FY89 and FY94

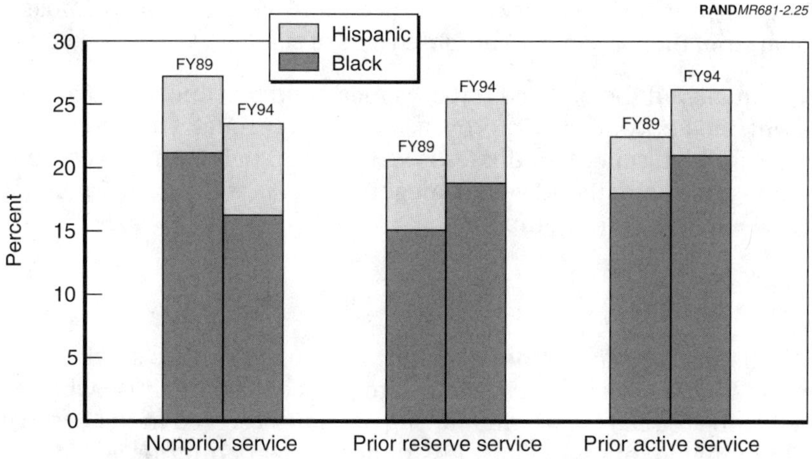

Figure 2.25—Percentage of Blacks and Hispanics Among Enlisted Gains, FY89 and FY94

or are returning to the reserve after a separation. The proportion of Hispanics in the enlisted gain cohorts has increased modestly over time.

SUMMARY

This chapter presented a profile of the Selected Reserve part-time enlisted inventory and enlisted gain cohorts and examined how this profile has changed over time from FY89 to FY94. Of particular interest are the changes in the proportion of prior-service personnel and the experience and quality of the enlisted force.

Inventory

The Reserve Components have increased their PS content by about 5 percentage points between FY89 and FY94, although the components differ markedly in their dependence on prior-service personnel. However, the numbers for ARNG point to the difficulty of meeting Title XI goals. Even factoring in the full-time personnel, the PS content of the ARNG in FY94 was 43 percent—far short of the 50 percent Congressionally mandated goal for the enlisted force.

The current force is very experienced and very senior. Almost a quarter of the force has 15 or more years of service.

The quality of the enlisted force, as measured by educational attainment and aptitude, has improved steadily over time. The percentage who are high school graduates is well over 85 percent in all components and the percentage of Category I–IIIA is well over 55 percent (70 percent in some components).

Gains

We distinguish three types of gains: NPS, prior reserve service; and prior active service. The middle category consists of those who are returning to the reserve after having previously served in the Reserve Components, but who have less than two years of prior active service; the other two were defined above. In FY89, PS gains accounted for about 30 percent of all accessions in the ARNG and USAR compared to 50–60 percent in the two Air Reserve Components. By FY93–FY94, PS gains have increased substantially as a proportion of all reserve gains.

The reserves are attracting more experienced PS personnel than they have in the past. The proportion of PS gains with 2–4 years of service has fallen dramatically from FY89 to FY94 and there has been a concomitant rise in the proportion with more than 6 years of service. The same shift toward taking in more experienced personnel is evident among prior-service gains as well.

The quality of the NPS enlisted gains is very high. Well over 90 percent of NPS gains have a high school diploma and there has been an increase of 1–10 percentage points in those scoring in the 50th percentile or above.

Table 2.1 summarizes the changes in the inventory profile over time.

We mentioned above that our definition of PS gains does not allow us to distinguish between those gained directly from the active force and those who had previously served in the active force but whose last service may well have been with a Reserve Component. These latter are counted as PS gains because they have two or more years of active service. Consequently, we have not directly addressed the question of whether the Reserve Components are being successful in recruiting from the larger pool of active force personnel created by the active force downsizing. To answer this question, we need to be able to identify accessions gained directly from the active force. We turn to this question next by looking at recent active-duty loss cohorts and examining their accession behavior.

Table 2.1

Summary of Changes in Inventory Profile, FY89–FY94

Selected Reserve Component	PS Inventory Content	Active-Duty Inventory Experience	Inventory Quality (HSG/CAT I–IIIA)
ARNG	Higher	Greater	Higher/Higher
USAR	Higher	Greater	Higher/Higher
NR	Higher	Greater	Higher/Stable
MCR	Higher	Greater	Higher/Higher
ANG	Higher	Greater	Higher/Higher
AFR	Higher	Greater	Higher/Stable

Chapter Three

THE TRANSITION OF PRIOR-SERVICE PERSONNEL FROM ACTIVE DUTY TO THE SELECTED RESERVE

A leading indicator of Selected Reserve problems is the reserves' success—or lack thereof—in attracting new prior-service personnel from the pool of individuals separating from the active force. These prior-service personnel enhance reserve readiness by enriching the experience base of the force and saving training resources. These savings are particularly large if the recruit is assigned a reserve position in his/her active-duty skill, since this job match maximizes the return on the recruit's experience and obviates the delay and cost associated with retraining.

After the drawdown, the Selected Reserve faces a potential crisis in personnel supply if the flow of new prior-service personnel is substantially reduced. In Grissmer et al. (1994b), we argued that the reserve would have difficulty maintaining the prior-service content of the pre-drawdown era, because the pipeline of prior-service personnel to the reserves would be disrupted by a disproportionate reduction in the active forces relative to the Selected Reserve forces. In the short term, the active force drawdown increased the number of separatees available to the reserve. It was unclear whether the reserve could capitalize on these large losses from the drawdown to enhance their prior-service content. Similarly, we were uncertain whether active-duty personnel affected by the drawdown might be less enthusiastic about affiliating with a Selected Reserve unit than those in the Cold War era had been. The changing roles, missions, and perceptions of the military and the Selected Reserve might also have changed the predisposition of departing active-duty personnel to affiliate with a reserve unit. In particular, the Selected Reserve deployment in ODS/S might have changed attitudes toward affiliation with a local reserve unit.

In this chapter, we examine the trends in new prior-service affiliations with the Selected Reserve:

- How well are the Reserve Components doing in attracting new prior-service personnel departing from the active force?
- Are the components succeeding in matching these prior-service personnel with their active-duty occupations?
- How long are new prior-service personnel staying in the Selected Reserve?

These factors are of critical importance for the reserve in maintaining readiness, because they affect the prior-service content of the force, the efficient use of prior-service experience, and ultimately the building blocks of the senior enlisted ranks in the Selected Reserve.

As background for our analysis, we begin by examining the size and progress of the active and reserve drawdown over the recent time period. The active drawdown, which began in 1992, has substantially decreased the size of the active forces. Operation Desert Shield/Storm delayed the planned active force drawdown, and the DoD stoploss policy during the Gulf War reduced active-duty separations to nearly zero in late 1990 and early 1991. As a result, the active force had relatively few losses in FY91 and an extraordinary number of losses in FY92. Table 3.1 shows that the active force drawdown has been the most severe in the Army, where enlisted endstrength has declined by 31 percent since FY89. The force reduction in the Air Force is the next largest at 26 percent. The size of the Navy declined by 22 percent, and the Marine Corps had the smallest decline in endstrength—12 percent between FY89 and FY94.

In addition, further cuts are planned through FY99. Army enlisted endstrength will stabilize at about 411,000 by FY96, which represents a decline of 9 percent over FY94 levels. Present plans call for a decline in Navy enlisted endstrength of 16.5 percent from the FY94 levels to 336,000. The Marine Corps endstrength will fall by a negligible 300 to 156,000, and the Air Force faces a further 11 percent reduction to an endstrength of 303,000 by FY99.

Table 3.1

Changes in Active-Duty Enlisted Endstrength by Service and Fiscal Year

FY	Army	Navy	Marine Corps	Air Force	Total
			Endstrength		
86	666668	504389	178615	494666	1844338
87	668410	510208	179478	495244	1853340
88	660445	515548	177271	466856	1820120
89	658321	515898	176857	462831	1813907
90	623519	502804	176694	430818	1733835
91	602777	495103	174287	409425	1681592
92	511335	468412	165397	375684	1520828
93	480379	439461	159949	356126	1435915
94	452513	402635	156335	341317	1352800
		Percentage Change in Endstrength Relative to FY89			
86	1.3	–2.2	1.0	6.9	1.7
87	1.5	–1.1	1.5	7.0	2.2
88	0.3	–0.0	0.2	0.9	0.3
89	0.0	0.0	0.0	0.0	0.0
90	–5.3	–2.5	–0.0	–6.9	–4.4
91	–8.4	–4.0	–1.5	–11.5	–7.3
92	–22.3	–9.2	–6.5	–18.8	–16.2
93	–27.0	–14.8	–9.6	–23.1	–20.8
94	–31.3	–22.0	–11.6	–26.3	–25.4

The Selected Reserve drawdown has differentially affected the Reserve Components. Table 3.2 shows the change in Selected Reserve enlisted endstrength by component. Reserve enlisted endstrength peaked in 1989 and has declined by about 15 percent since then. This pattern varies somewhat across components. The decline has been most dramatic in the Naval Reserve where strength levels have declined by 30 percent relative to their 1989 levels. The reserve drawdown has also had large effects on the two Army components with the Army National Guard and Army Reserve declining by 14 and 20 percent, respectively. The Marine Corps Reserve and Air components had much smaller reductions in strength.

Table 3.2

Changes in Selected Reserve Endstrength by Component and Fiscal Year

FY	ARNG	USAR	NR	MCR	ANG	USAFR	Total
			Endstrength				
86	402628	253070	116640	38123	99231	62505	972197
87	406487	255291	121938	38721	100827	63855	987119
88	406966	253467	121653	39930	101261	65567	988844
89	406848	256872	122537	39948	101980	66126	994311
90	394060	248326	123117	40903	103637	66566	976609
91	395988	249626	123727	41472	103670	67603	982086
92	378904	245135	115341	38748	104758	65806	948692
93	363263	219610	105254	38092	102920	64720	893859
94	351390	206849	86300	36860	99711	63411	844521
			Percentage Change in Endstrength Relative to FY89				
86	–1.0	–1.5	–4.8	–4.6	–2.7	–5.5	–2.2
87	–0.1	–0.6	–0.5	–3.1	–1.1	–3.4	–0.7
88	0.0	–1.3	–0.7	0.0	–0.7	–0.8	–0.5
89	0.0	0.0	0.0	0.0	0.0	0.0	0.0
90	–3.1	–3.3	0.5	2.4	1.6	0.7	–1.8
91	–2.7	–2.8	1.0	3.8	1.7	2.2	–1.2
92	–6.9	–4.6	–5.9	–3.0	2.7	–0.5	–4.6
93	–10.7	–14.5	–14.1	–4.6	0.9	–2.1	–10.1
94	–13.6	–19.5	–29.6	–7.7	–2.2	–4.1	–15.1

The reserve drawdown means that the demand for new personnel was weaker in the past few years than during the period from FY86 through FY89 when reserve endstrenth was relatively stable or increasing. Although all components are shrinking somewhat, the declines are most pronounced in the NR and USAR. On the other hand, the supply of prior-service personnel available to the Selected Reserve has been unusually large in the past few years.

As with the active force, further reductions in Selected Reserve endstrength of about 11 percent are planned. As Figure 3.1 shows, the components will be differentially affected by the planned cuts, with the USAR being hit the hardest. ARNG endstrength will decline by 8

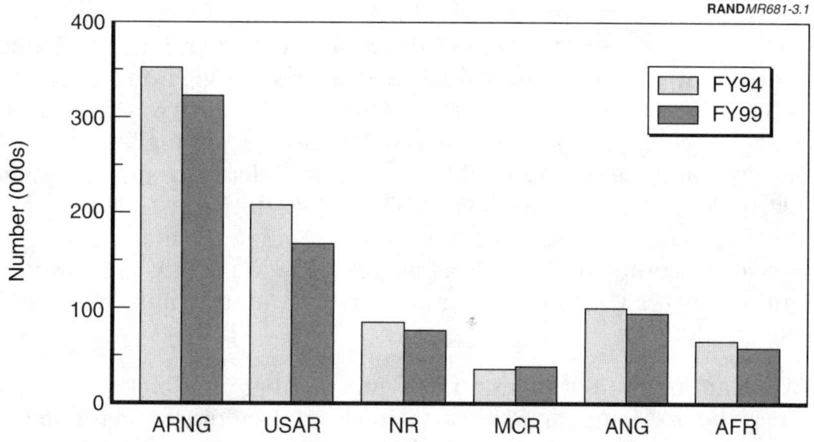

Figure 3.1—Selected Reserve Enlisted Endstrength by Component, FY94 and FY99

percent from FY94 to FY99 to 323,349, and the USAR endstrength will be cut by about 19 percent from approximately 207,000 in FY94 to 168,000 by FY99. NR faces a decline in endstrength of about 12 percent, whereas the Air Reserve Components face somewhat smaller cuts: 7 percent (ANG) and 9 percent (AFR). No cuts are planned for the Marine Corps Reserve.

In this chapter, we focus on individuals who were released from active service at the expiration of their term of service (ETS) or who were released as part of an early release program. These individuals constitute the prime prior active service market available to the Selected Reserve Components. Other active-duty separatees are attrition losses, and their separation conditions frequently limit eligibility for joining the Selected Reserve. In some cases, special waivers allow an individual who was discharged from the active force for medical or behavioral problems to affiliate with the reserve. Nevertheless, the vast majority of new affiliates come from the group of individuals who satisfactorily complete their active-duty terms (Buddin and Kirin, 1994; Marquis and Kirby, 1989).

The analysis examines two groups of active-duty losses: junior personnel with 2–6 years of active-duty experience and mid-career personnel with 7–12 years of active-duty experience. These two groups correspond to individuals who have served one term in the active force (or possibly have reenlisted once or have extended their initial enlistment) and those individuals who are separating from the career force. The two groups are treated separately, because we anticipated that the groups might have different interests in joining the Selected Reserve, and the reserve might have different demands for personnel with different experience levels. The active-duty retirement system provides a strong incentive for individuals with more than 12 years of service to complete 20 years of service and earn a pension, so there are few losses with 13–20 years of service and we will not examine that group.

We examine both affiliation rates and number of affiliations to address the first issue raised above. However, it should be clear that total affiliations are the result of the interaction of supply and demand arising from unit vacancies in the Reserve Components and do not merely reflect the propensities of prior-service personnel to enlist in the reserves. As a result, one needs to be cautious when drawing inferences from these trends, particularly during periods of drawdown.

SELECTED RESERVE AFFILIATIONS WITHIN ONE YEAR OF ACTIVE-DUTY SERVICE

Prior active service personnel are most likely to join Selected Reserve units in the first few months after they leave the active force. Active force personnel meet with in-service personnel counselors as they complete their active tours, and these counselors advise personnel who plan to leave on opportunities available in Selected Reserve units. Interested individuals might affiliate with a reserve unit immediately or might wait until visiting local facilities after returning home from active duty. Although some individuals affiliate later if their personal circumstances change, previous research (Buddin and Kirin, 1994; Marquis and Kirby, 1989) has shown that most affiliations occur in the first few months after leaving the active force and the vast majority occur in the year following separation. For now, we will focus on affiliations in this first year after leaving the active force, but in the next section, we will examine trends in the timing of affiliation.[1]

Active Army Losses and Affiliations

Figure 3.2 shows the trends in the number of active Army losses and one-year affiliation rates of personnel leaving the Army from FY86 through FY93. We focus on the ARNG and USAR because very few active Army separatees join a non–Army Reserve Component.

The pattern of active Army losses is dominated by the stoploss policy during Operation Desert Shield/Storm and the subsequent Army drawdown. Losses in FY91 are unusually small, and losses in FY92 are unusually large, especially for mid-career personnel. The FY92 losses for mid-career enlisted personnel were about three times those of previous and subsequent cohorts.

Among junior personnel, the overall affiliation rate has been stable over the eight years, but the composition of reserve gains has shifted from the USAR to the ARNG. In FY86, 12 and 29 percent of junior Army losses joined the ARNG and USAR, respectively. In FY93, the total affiliation rate was somewhat higher than in FY86 (44 percent compared with 41 percent), but the composition had shifted dramatically: The ARNG attracted 26 percent of separatees, compared with 18 percent for the USAR. We can speculate as to the reasons: Perhaps the ARNG had more vacancies or had a policy of overmanning, or individuals preferred ARNG to USAR because of

[1]The analysis of affiliation trends focuses on an equal period of opportunity for individuals to join the reserves. A priori, we would expect that the probability of affiliation (for any one individual) would decrease with the number of months since leaving active duty but that the total number of affiliations would rise. If we did not control for this window of opportunity, we could be misled by the observed rates. For example, suppose that 25 percent of the FY86 active-duty loss cohort had affiliated with a reserve unit by the end of FY94 compared with 20 percent of the FY93 cohort. Although the rate is higher for FY86 than for FY93, the earlier cohort had up to nine years to affiliate compared with only two years for the FY93 cohort. In this chapter, we compare the one-year affiliation rates of the two cohorts, so we can make more balanced assessments of whether the affiliation trend is improving or worsening. The comparison admittedly begs the supply question. If there are a large number of separatees and a smaller number of available positions, a low number of affiliations in the first year could by itself be misleading.

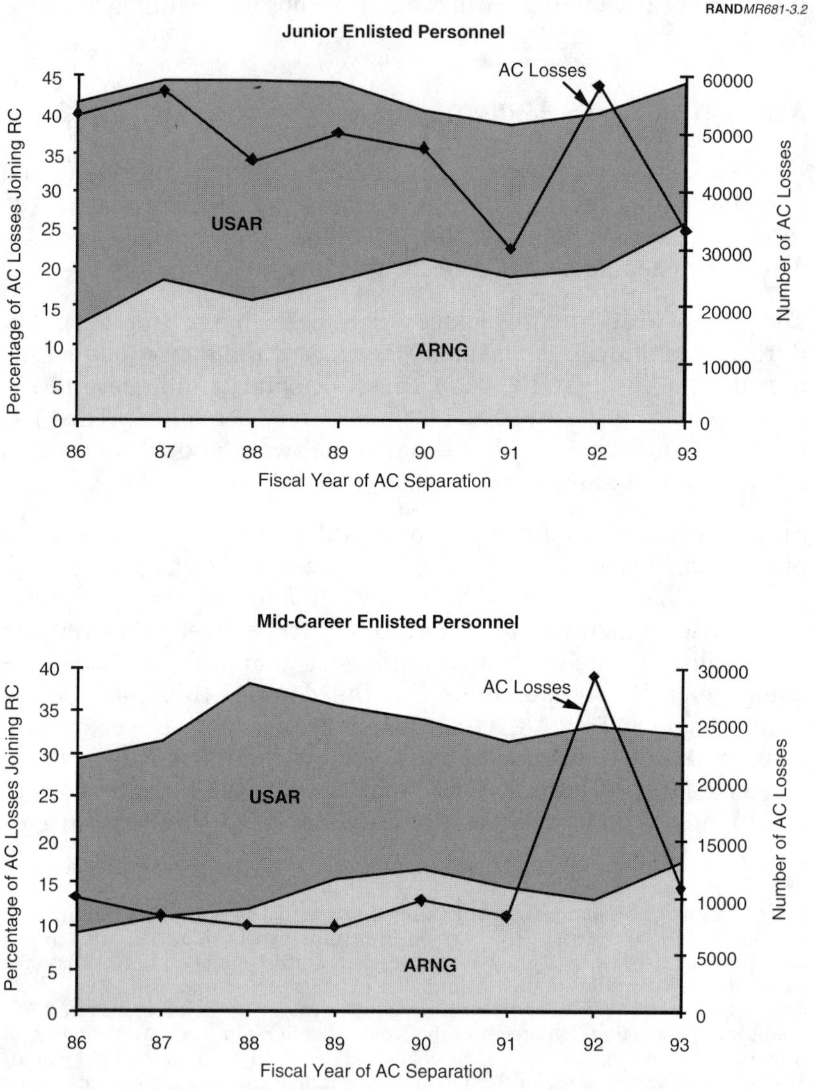

Figure 3.2—Trends in Active Army Separations and Selected Reserve Affiliations, FY86–FY93

inherent differences between the two components, or the Guard gave preferential treatment to PS individuals.

The affiliation patterns for mid-career personnel are similar, but the overall affiliation rate among mid-career personnel has been somewhat lower in most years. About 29 percent of the FY86 loss cohort joined the reserve, and over two-thirds affiliated with the USAR. The overall affiliation rate improved to 38 percent in FY88, but the rate has declined to 32 percent in FY93. By FY93, the share of affiliations attributable to the USAR has fallen to 47 percent.

The stability of the overall affiliation rate means that the Army Reserve Components have succeeded in capturing unusually large numbers of prior-service personnel from the drawdown, and this was partly reflected in the higher proportions of PS gains reported in Chapter Two. In the case of mid-career personnel, the ARNG and USAR absorbed nearly three times as many new prior-service gains from the FY92 cohort as from previous Army loss cohorts. Junior losses in FY92 were also considerably larger than those of the FY88 through FY90 cohorts, so the number of junior-level affiliations increased by about 20 percent.

The sustained overall affiliation rate among Army losses and the success in attracting losses during the drawdown are promising signs for the Army Reserve Components.

Active Navy Losses and Affiliations

The pattern of active force losses in the Navy is somewhat different from that of the Army during the drawdown. First, Table 3.1 shows that the Navy decline was 22 percent compared with 31 percent in the Army. Second, the Army drawdown was very concentrated in the FY92 cohort, whereas the Navy decline was spread more evenly across the FY92, FY93, and FY94 cohorts.

Figure 3.3 shows the patterns of Navy losses and subsequent affiliations with the NR. Nearly all Navy losses who affiliate with a Selected Reserve unit join the NR (rather than another Reserve Component), so the analysis will focus on these affiliations.

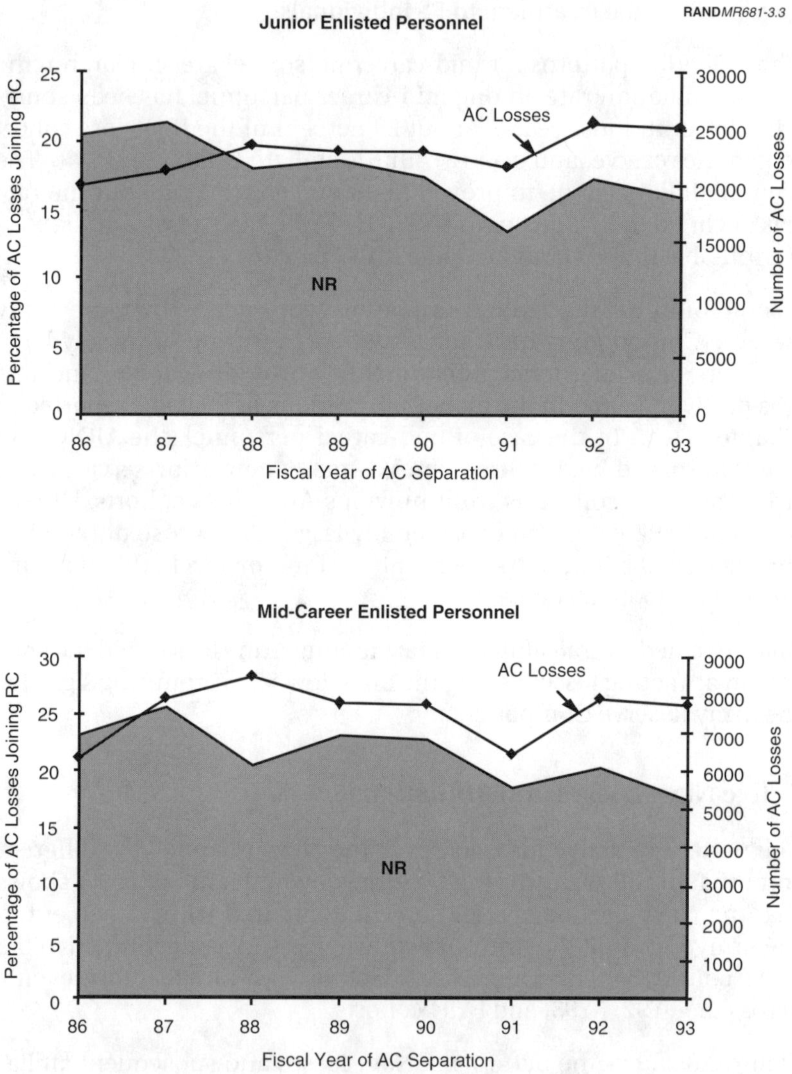

Figure 3.3—Trends in Active Navy Separations and Selected Reserve Affiliations, FY86–FY93

The affiliation rate of both junior and mid-career separatees has fallen off somewhat from the rates of the late 1980s. The affiliation rate of junior personnel has fallen from 20 percent in FY86 to 16 percent in FY93. Mid-career-level affiliations have fallen from 23 percent to 17 percent between FY86 and FY93. The declining rates are applied to a larger base number of losses in the recent cohorts, however, so the total number of affiliations with the NR has increased slightly among junior personnel and has declined by about 10 percent for mid-career personnel. Junior-level losses and NR gains are about three times as large as for mid-career personnel.

Declining NR affiliation rates might well reflect the limited availability of positions in the NR. As discussed above, the NR is ramping down its endstrength substantially, so Navy losses might have difficulties finding NR positions to fill.

Active Marine Corps Losses and Affiliations

The MCR has traditionally had very few prior-service personnel as a matter of policy, perhaps because of its primarily combat mission. The enlisted ranks of the MCR are drawn predominantly from non-prior-service personnel and affiliations from the MCR to the USMC are more common than those from the USMC to the MCR. The limited MCR demand for prior-service personnel is an important factor in the decision of many Marine Corps personnel to affiliate with other Selected Reserve Components (primarily the ARNG and less often the USAR). In all service branches except the Marine Corps, the overwhelmingly dominant flow of prior-service reserve affiliations comes from the corresponding active service.

The overall probability of Selected Reserve affiliation is smaller for Marine Corps personnel than for those from any other service branch. In FY93, the affiliation rates for junior personnel from the Army, Navy, and Air Force were 44, 16, and 33 percent, respectively, compared with only 11 percent for junior-level Marines. This low affiliation rate may well reflect the fact that in-service USMC recruiters have few MCR positions to fill. Nonetheless, the pool of USMC personnel is a potential resource for ARNG and USAR units that need prior-service personnel in related job skills.

The MCR affiliation rate has declined somewhat over recent cohorts but the small flow of USMC personnel to other Selected Reserve Components has been relatively stable (see Figure 3.4). The large MCR decline in affiliations in FY91 is probably an anomaly related to ODS/S—recruiters could not recruit for units that were mobilized during ODS/S.

Among junior personnel, the MCR affiliation rate has fallen from 10 percent in FY86 to 7 percent in FY93. Affiliations in other Reserve Components have been stable at about 4 percent. Junior losses were unusually high in FY92 and FY93, so more USMC personnel were joining reserve units in these years despite the low rates of affiliation.

Mid-career losses are only about 20 percent as large as junior losses, but the pattern of affiliations has been similar for the two groups. The affiliation rate for mid-career personnel has fallen from 10 percent to 7 percent in the MCR, whereas the rate has risen from 6 to 7 percent for all other Reserve Components.

Active Air Force Losses and Affiliations

The active Air Force drawdown actually began in FY86 as the Air Force began reducing its endstrength. These reductions involved management actions to allow special early release programs in FY88 and FY90. FY92 also produced a big loss cohort for mid-career Air Force personnel as part of a broader OSD-level attempt to reduce endstrength.

These special management actions induced an unusual pattern in Air Force losses between FY86 and FY93. Figure 3.5 shows that the FY88 and FY90 loss cohorts were unusual large for both mid-career and junior personnel. The early releases meant that the FY89 and FY91 loss cohorts were unusually small (FY91 losses were mitigated by stoploss as well), since many individuals who would have normally left in these year groups had already left early. The high mid-career losses in FY92 were the result of special OSD-sponsored programs to thin out the mid-career enlisted force as part of the drawdown.

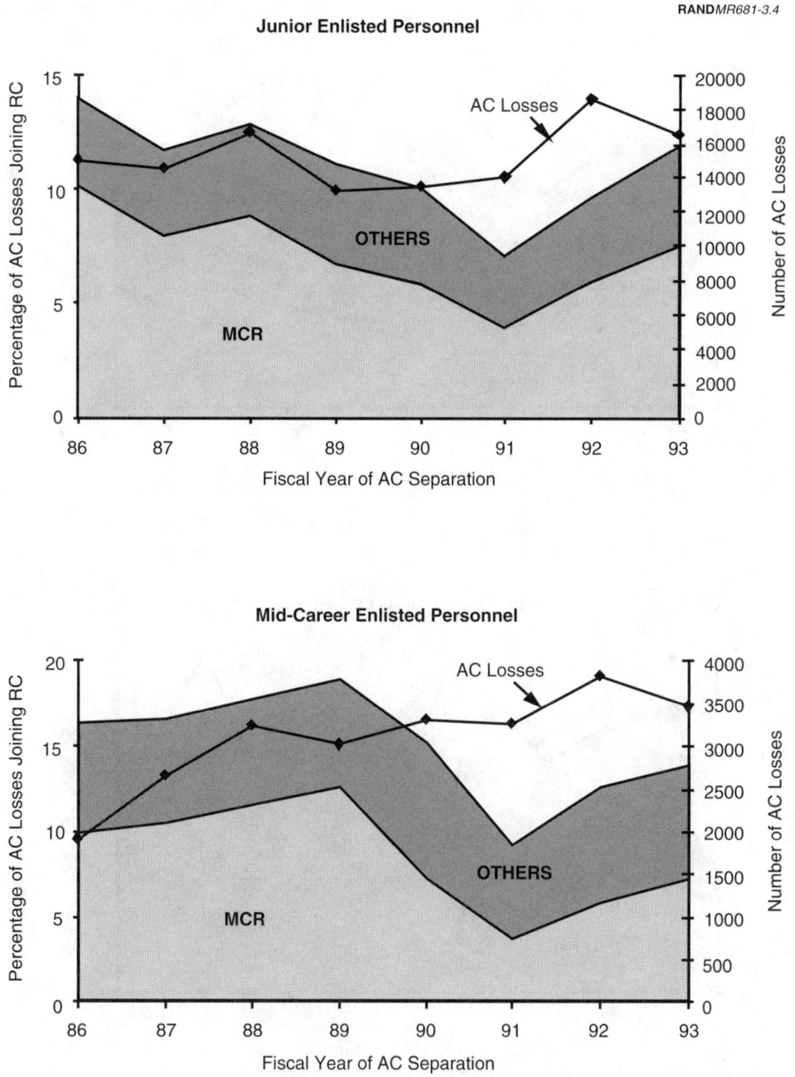

Figure 3.4—Trends in Active Marine Corps Separations and Selected Reserve Affiliations, FY86–FY93

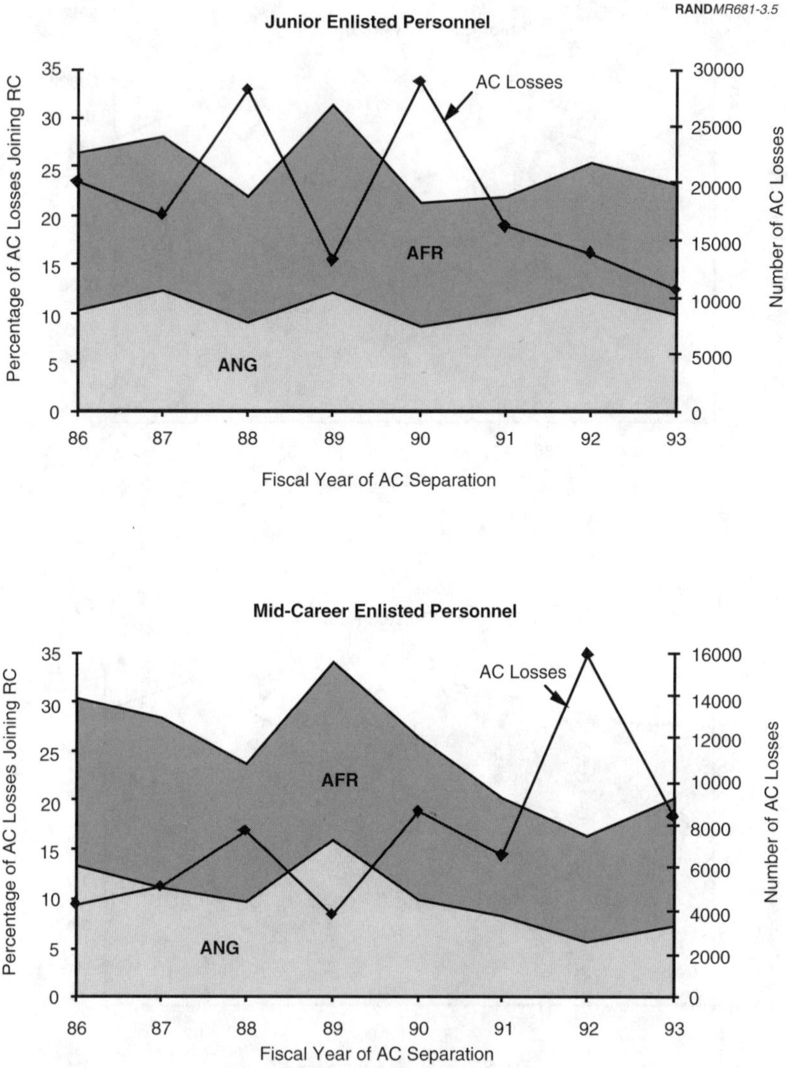

Figure 3.5—Trends in Active Air Force Separations and Selected Reserve Affiliations, FY86–FY93

The overall affiliation rate of Air Force personnel has varied somewhat over time, but the trend is slightly downward.[2] The affiliation rate for junior personnel was 26 percent in FY86 and has fallen to 23 percent in FY93. The affiliation rate has been very responsive to the size of the respective loss cohorts: The affiliation rate was low in FY88 and FY90 when the losses were high but was high in FY89 when the losses were low. This relationship between affiliations and losses reflects the fact that the Air Reserve Components are well staffed with prior-service personnel and have low attrition rates (Grissmer et al., 1994b), so the Air Reserve Components have fewer positions to fill than other components do.

Mid-career affiliation rates have declined substantially, from 30 percent in FY86 to 20 percent in FY93. As with junior personnel, the affiliation rates and number of losses move in opposite directions, so large loss cohorts are associated with small affiliation rates and vice versa.

The composition of the declines in affiliation rates has varied somewhat between the ANG and AFR. For junior personnel, the ANG rates have been fairly stable over time, and the overall reduction reflects a 3 percentage point reduction in the AFR affiliation rate. For mid-career personnel, the 10 percentage point reduction in the overall affiliation rate has been divided among the ANG (6 percentage points) and the AFR (4 percentage points).

THE TIMING OF SELECTED RESERVE AFFILIATION AFTER LEAVING ACTIVE DUTY

In this section, we will examine how the time to join a Selected Reserve unit has changed in recent cohorts. This analysis is important, because changes in the timing of affiliation might distort the trends observed in one-year affiliation rates. For example, a stable one-year rate might mask substantial cohort differences in reserve participation if affiliations were more concentrated in the early months in some cohorts than in others. However, affiliation rates may be demand-constrained because of the lack of immediate

[2]Again, as we cautioned above, trends in affiliation rates can be misleading as indicators of trends in the propensity to enlist when demand is constrained.

vacancies and one-year affiliation rates may not accurately reflect the supply of prior-service personnel willing to join the reserve. Therefore, we need to be cautious when interpreting these trends.

Figure 3.6 shows that the Army Reserve Components have improved their affiliation rates for both junior and mid-career personnel. At the junior level, immediate (same-quarter) affiliations with the reserve improved from 19 percent in FY86 to 25 and 27 percent, respectively, in FY89 and FY93. The affiliation rate for the FY93 cohort has remained above that of the earlier cohorts for each respective time period. The cumulative affiliation rate after seven quarters for the FY93 cohort[3] is comparable to that of the twelve-quarter rate for the earlier cohorts.

Mid-career Army losses in FY93 have a higher direct affiliation rate with the reserve than did the FY86 cohort but a lower rate than that for the FY89 cohort. The strong performance of the FY93 cohort is evidenced by the fact that the most recent cumulative affiliation rate for the FY93 cohort is 39 percent after seven quarters as compared with lower overall rates for the earlier cohorts after twelve quarters.

Figure 3.6 shows that initial Navy affiliations have been comparable across cohorts, but the cumulative rates do not rise as rapidly in the FY93 cohort as in the pre-drawdown years. At this point, the cumulative affiliation rates for the Navy are running 1 and 3 percentage points behind that of the FY89 cohort. These changes in the cumulative rates are somewhat smaller than the declines in one-year affiliation rates.

The affiliation rates for USMC losses reflect substantial gains to components other than the MCR (see Figure 3.7). An important feature of the rates is that they start very low for initial affiliations but then continue to rise substantially over time. For junior personnel, the affiliation rate is nearly as high during the second year after active-duty separation as during the first. The cumulative affiliation rate for the FY93 cohort is 19 percent after seven quarters as compared with rates of 18 and 16 percent for the FY86 and FY89 cohorts,

[3]The twelve-quarter affiliation rate for the FY93 cohort will not be known until FY96. The seven-quarter rate is for FY93 losses tracked through the end of FY94.

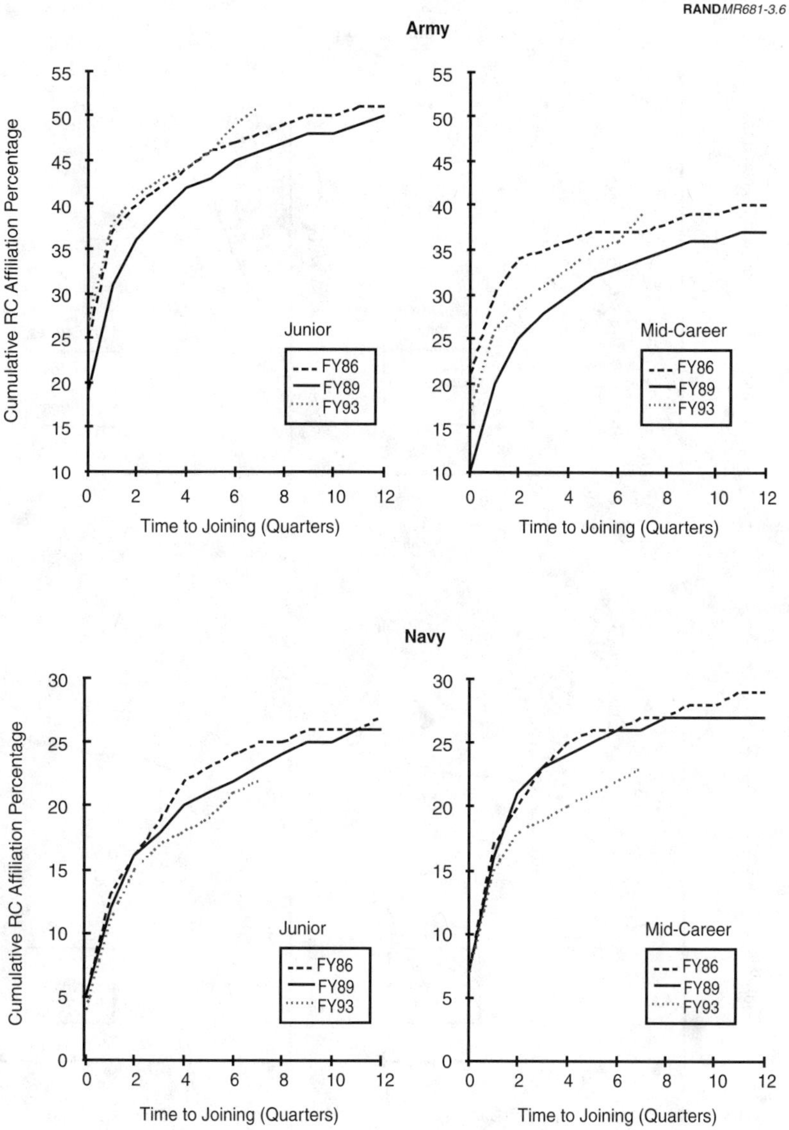

Figure 3.6—Timing of Selected Reserve Affiliation for Active Army and Navy Losses, FY86, FY89, and FY93

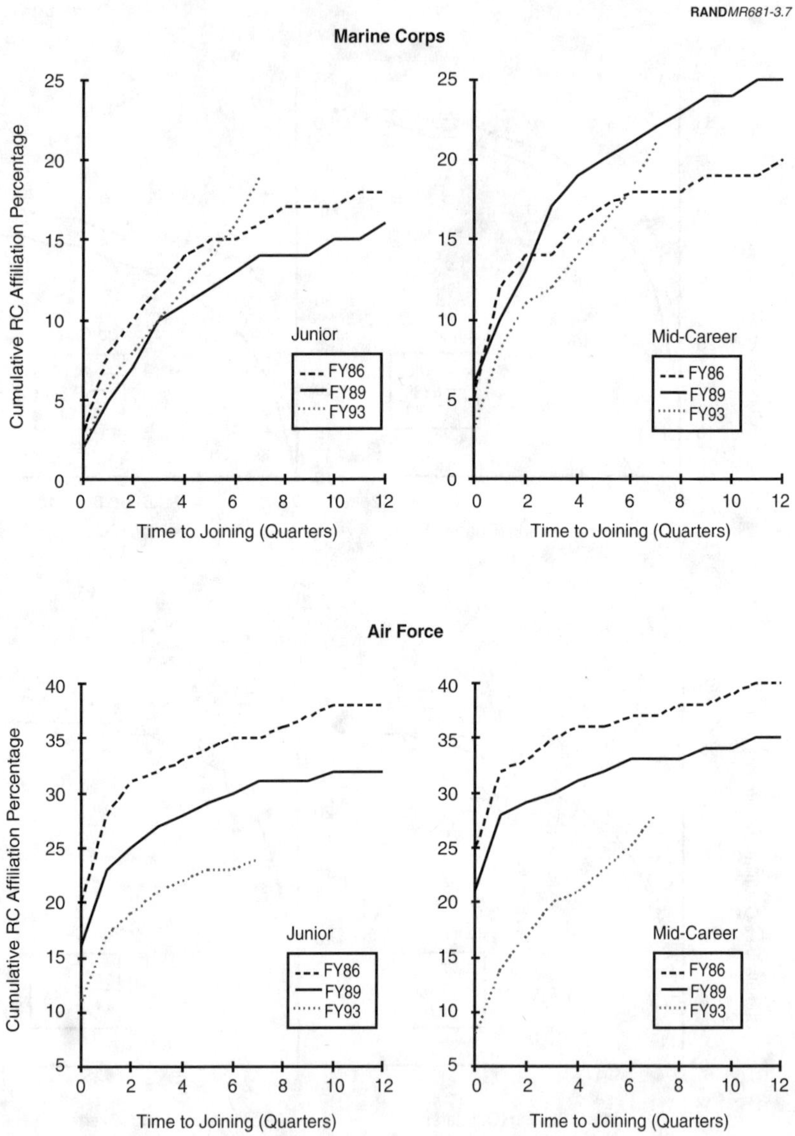

Figure 3.7—Timing of Selected Reserve Affiliation for Active Marine Corps and Air Force Losses, FY86, FY89, and FY93

respectively, after twelve quarters. The timing information shows that although one-year affiliations are down, the FY93 cohort is actually producing a somewhat higher cumulative affiliation percentage over time than the earlier cohorts did.

The cumulative attrition rates for mid-career Marine Corps losses are typically lower than those for the earlier cohorts. As with junior-level Marines, the rates increase substantially into the second year after active-duty separation.

The cumulative affiliation rates for Air Force separatees vary substantially by cohort (see Figure 3.7). Among both junior and mid-career losses, the initial and cumulative rates were highest for the FY89 cohort and lowest for the FY93 cohort. The timing results for the Air Force largely mirror the results for one-year affiliations.

JOB MATCH RATES OF NEW PRIOR-SERVICE PERSONNEL IN THE SELECTED RESERVE

Selected Reserve units will enhance the value of prior-service personnel in their units by matching individuals' active-duty and reserve job assignments. Unmatched members will need retraining for their reserve positions. This retraining is costly and will delay the member in becoming fully proficient at the new job assignment (Buddin and Grissmer, 1994).

The job matching problem is largely unique to the reserve. In the active force, personnel are trained to fill unit openings and then are moved to available positions. Some shortfalls and overages will occur, but the training base trains personnel full-time and assigns them to disparate units. A Selected Reserve unit must recruit personnel in its vicinity to fill openings in the unit. In some cases, prior-service personnel might not have the job skills required in the local unit, and only distant units might have positions available that match the soldier's active-duty job. Units must fill some vacancies with non-matched prior-service personnel and then train the new member in the assigned job. Alternatively, the unit might forgo the mismatched prior-service soldier, recruit a nonprior-service member for the unit, and send the recruit to basic and initial skill training in the required job.

High job match rates may not be a panacea for the reserve, because they may reflect a very restricted management policy. Other things equal, the reserve would always prefer to match new prior-service recruits with unit vacancies. Unfortunately, prior-service individuals with the appropriate job skills in that geographical area might be in short supply, so the unit vacancy might remain unfilled for some time if the unit insists on a job match. Similarly, the affiliation rate might be artificially depressed if interested prior-service personnel are discouraged from joining the unit because their job skills are not needed there.

Initial Job Match Rates of Prior-Service Personnel in ARNG and USAR

At the junior ranks, the ARNG has made dramatic progress in improving its job match rate (see Figure 3.8); the match rate improved from 42 percent in FY86 to 65 percent in FY93.[4] The USAR match rate rose in the late 1980s, then fell in the early 1990s, and the FY93 level is nearly the same as that in FY86. These changes mean that the 30 percentage point advantage of the USAR in job match has narrowed to only 6 percentage points in FY93.

The ARNG and USAR might have improved their job match marks in FY92 when the large loss cohort would have allowed them more discretion in filling vacancies. This did not occur (at least partly due to strength or need constraints), but the components did sustain fairly high match rates (relative to historical standards in the ARNG) and absorbed a much larger number of junior-level gains.

Among mid-career personnel, the USAR has been consistently better than the ARNG at matching new prior-service personnel with their active-duty jobs. The ARNG has improved its match rate over time and the rate has declined in the USAR, so the gap between the two components has narrowed from 20 percentage points in FY86 to 10 percentage points in FY93. The USAR match rate for mid-career personnel has varied considerable over these few years from 72 percent in FY88 to only 59 percent in FY90.

---

[4]Possible overmanning in some ARNG units during this period may have contributed to the higher match rate.

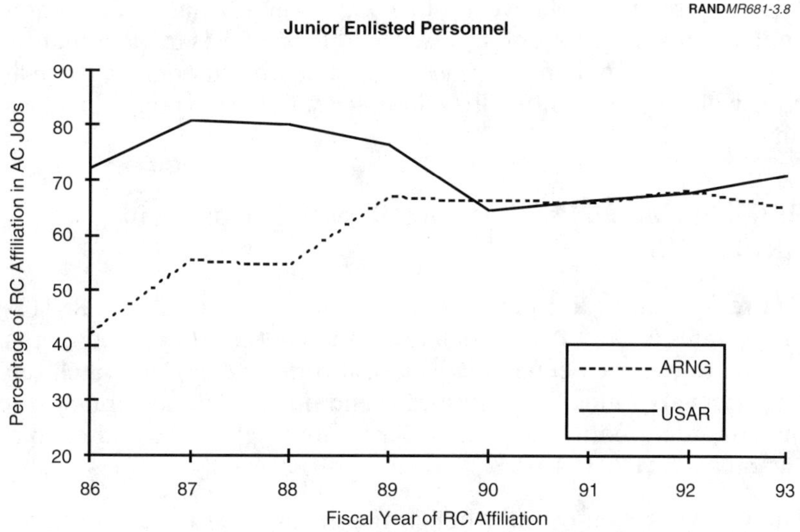

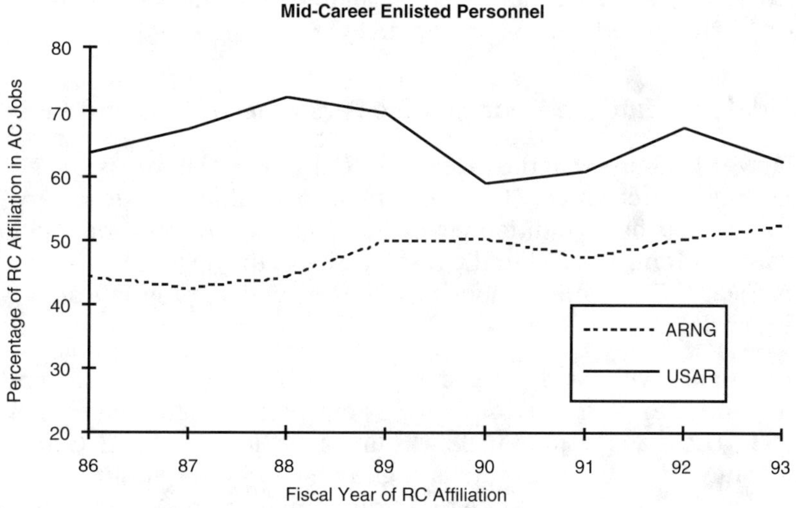

Figure 3.8—Percentage of ARNG and USAR Prior-Service Gains Assigned in Their Active-Duty Job Skill, FY86–FY93

Mid-career personnel have a somewhat lower job match rate in both components than do junior personnel. This reflects the fact that the job matching problems increase with rank and experience, since an NCO will have more difficulties finding a suitable job match in a local unit.

Initial Job Match Rates of Prior-Service Personnel in NR and MCR

Figure 3.9 shows the job match rates for the NR and MCR. The match rates in the NR are much lower than in the other components, but the rates have been rising in recent cohorts. The NR match rate does not vary much between junior and mid-career personnel—the match rate for both groups was 35 percent in FY86 and had risen to 46 percent by FY93.

The match rates for junior personnel in the MCR have been more volatile than those of mid-career personnel, but the overall trend has been toward improvement. For junior personnel, the match rate was 58 percent in FY86 and improved to 63 percent in FY93.

The numbers of new mid-career affiliates are small, but the match rate has improved from 54 percent in FY86 to 63 percent in FY93.

Initial Job Match of Prior-Service Personnel in ANG and AFR

Figure 3.10 shows that the Air Reserve Components have historically had high match rates. This reflects, in part, that the Air Reserve Components have traditionally had long queues of active-duty personnel wishing to enlist in the reserve and so the ANG and AFR may have some discretion in choosing members with appropriate active-duty skills.

The junior-level match rates have improved for both the ANG and the AFR. The ANG rates rose from 54 percent in FY86 to 69 percent in FY93. The match rate in FY92 was unusually low for the ANG at 51 percent. The job match rate is slightly higher in the AFR than the ANG, and the AFR match rate rose from 65 percent in FY86 to 70 percent in FY93.

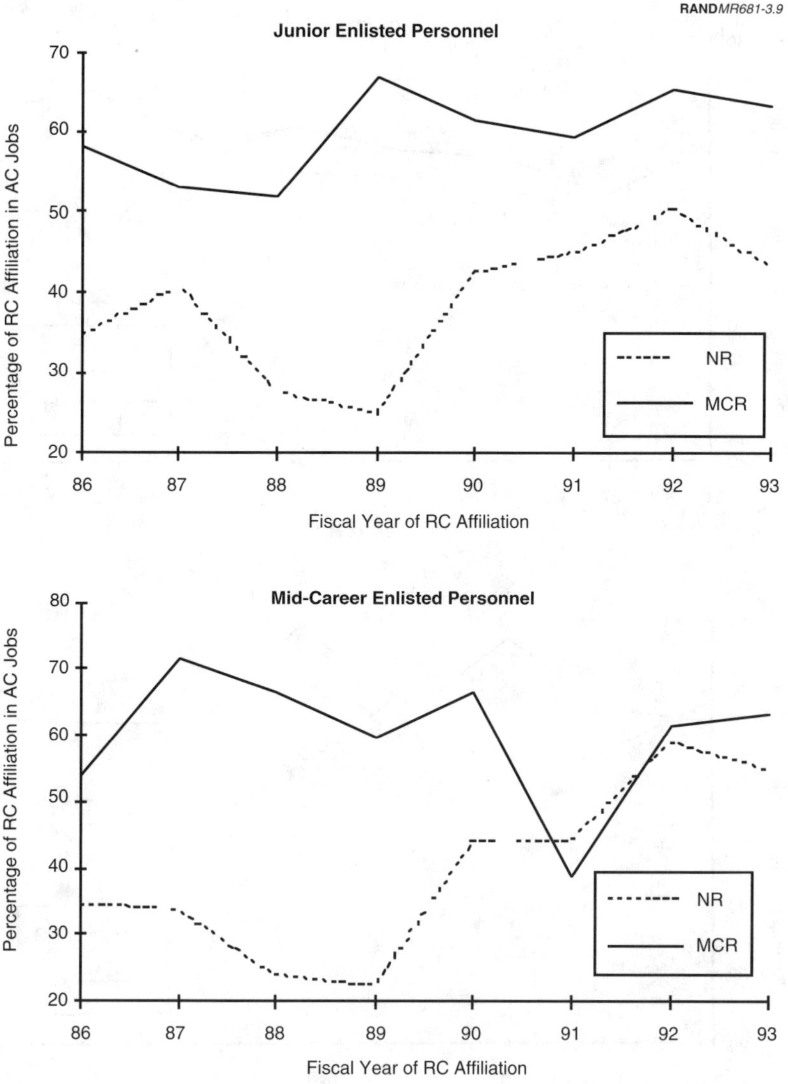

Figure 3.9—Percentage of NR and MCR Prior-Service Gains Assigned in Their Active-Duty Job Skill, FY86–FY93

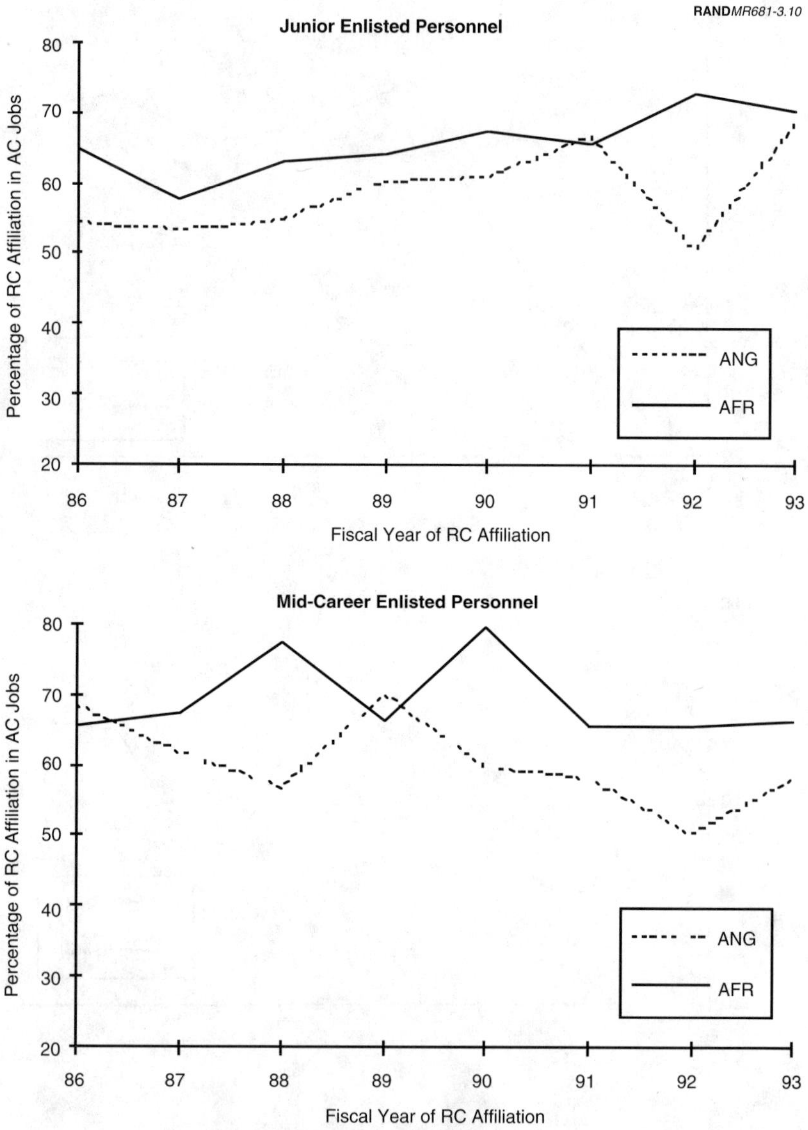

Figure 3.10—Percentage of ANG and AFR Prior-Service Gains Assigned in Their Active-Duty Job Skill, FY86–FY93

Mid-career match rates have declined substantially for the ANG since FY86, but the rates for the AFR are unchanged. In the ANG, the job match rate declined from 68 percent in FY86 to 58 percent in FY93. Match rates in the AFR have been volatile, but the FY86 rate of 66 percent was equivalent to that in FY93. A possible explanation for the sharp changes in the match rate from FY87 through FY91 is the large swings in active Air Force losses because of early-release programs. The AFR might have achieved higher match rates from the large loss cohorts in FY88 and FY90 because they could select from among a larger cohort of losses to fill unit vacancies. However, this fails to explain why a corresponding "spike" did not occur in the AFR match rate in FY92 when the mid-career loss cohort was also large as a result of special drawdown programs.

FIRST-YEAR RESERVE ATTRITION FOR NEW PRIOR-SERVICE GAINS

How long do new gains remain in the Selected Reserve? This section examines the first-year attrition behavior of those individuals who affiliate with a reserve unit. Gains in reserve affiliation would provide little long-term benefit if they were offset by higher reserve attrition. Alternatively, a stable affiliation rate would yield increased prior-service content for the component if the attrition rate were reduced and the period of reserve participation were increased. In the next section, we will examine the longer-term flows of prior-service personnel exiting the reserve and later returning. For now, the analysis will focus on whether new prior-service affiliates complete a year of reserve service without a break in service.

Figure 3.11 shows that the ARNG attrition rate has fallen substantially for both junior and mid-career personnel. Junior-level attrition has fallen from 25 percent in FY86 to 14 percent in FY93. Among new mid-career members, first-year attrition has been somewhat erratic, with much higher loss rates in FY86, FY89, and FY90 than in the other years. The post-ODS/S attrition rates for mid-career personnel have been 8 to 10 percentage points lower than for the earlier years.

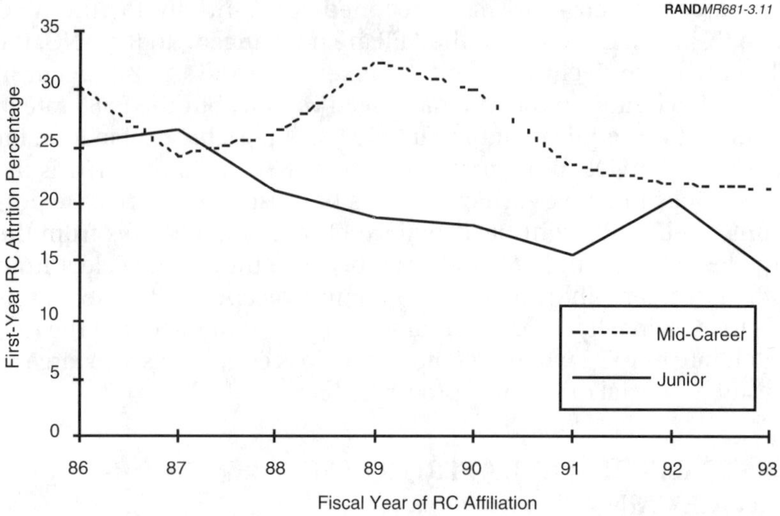

Figure 3.11—Trends in First-Year Attrition Rates of New Prior-Service Gains to the ARNG, FY86–FY93

The first-year attrition rates for new prior-service gains in the USAR were quite high in FY86, but the rates have fallen substantially since then (see Figure 3.12). In FY86, the attrition rates for new junior and mid-career personnel were 46 and 35 percent, respectively. The mid-career rate rose to 48 percent in FY87. Although the attrition rates remain much higher than for ARNG units,[5] the rates have declined to 27 and 33 percent for junior and mid-career personnel, respectively, in FY93. Even with the recent improvements, the USAR has a substantial problem retaining the new prior-service personnel that it attracts.

[5]The lower attrition of new affiliates in Guard units than in reserve units may reflect several factors. First, several states offer special benefits to Guard members, and these benefits may lower attrition. These benefits may also signal a pattern of community support for the Guard that eases employer and family conflicts associated with Guard participation. Second, missions and jobs differ substantially across Guard/reserve units, and these differences may make Guard positions more interesting or challenging to new affiliates. In a future analysis, we will develop a multivariate model of attrition and attempt to identify the underlying factors associated with these differences.

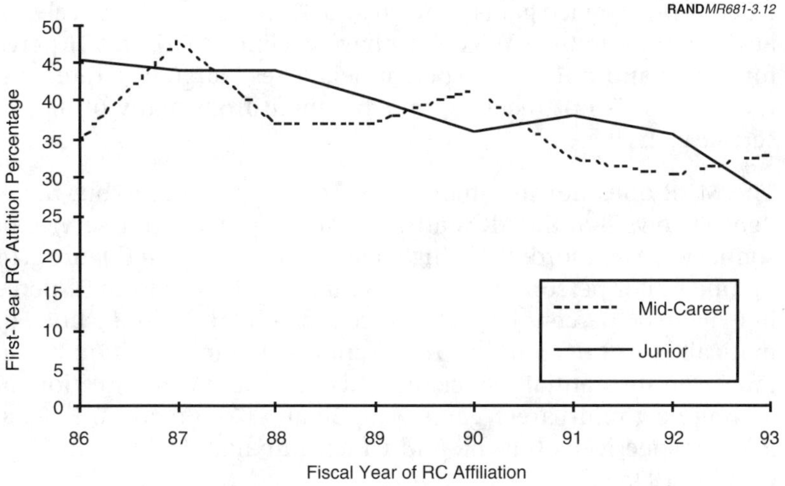

Figure 3.12—Trends in First-Year Attrition Rates of New Prior-Service Gains to the USAR, FY86–FY93

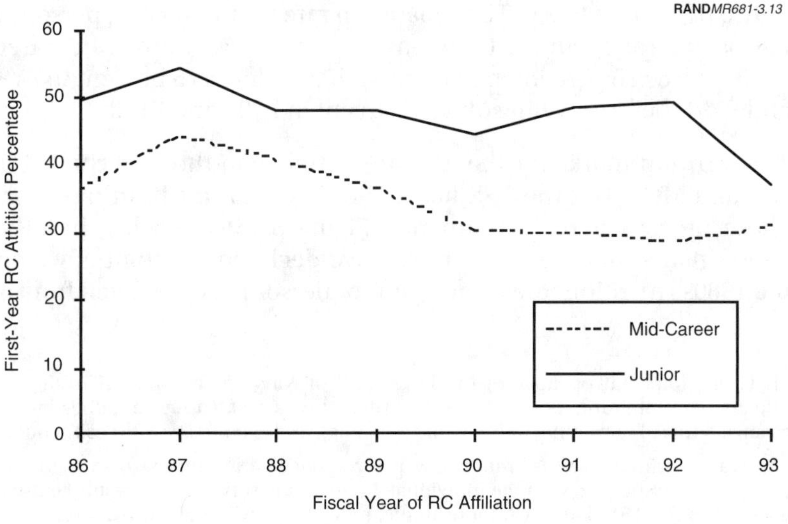

Figure 3.13—Trends in First-Year Attrition Rates of New Prior-Service Gains to the NR, FY86–FY93

career prior-service gains were 50 and 37 percent, respectively. The attrition rates in the FY93 cohort have declined to 37 and 31 percent for junior and mid-career personnel. These large loss rates mean that the NR is not receiving much benefit from many of its prior-service gains.[6]

The MCR does not use many prior-service personnel, but the evidence shows that the MCR attrition rates for new prior-service personnel were extraordinarily high before the drawdown (Figure 3.14).[7] Among junior personnel, the first-year loss rate rose from 62 percent in FY86 to 66 percent in FY88. Since then, the rate has declined dramatically to 23 percent in FY93. Senior personnel attrition has also improved substantially since the end of the Cold War. Attrition rates among new mid-career gains were 50 and 62 percent in FY86 and FY87, respectively, but the mid-career rate had declined to 33 percent in FY93.

The ANG has historically had much lower first-year attrition than any of the other components, and the ANG has substantially reduced this loss rate since the end of the Cold War (Figure 3.15). Among junior personnel, the attrition rate has fallen from 17 percent in FY86 to only 6 percent in FY93. The separation rate for mid-career personnel has been erratic, but the trend has also been downward. Mid-career attrition was 16 percent in FY86 and fell to as low as 5 percent in FY90 and FY91, before leveling off at 9 percent in FY92 and FY93.

The attrition marks for the AFR are better than those of the USAR, NR, and MCR, but the AFR has higher first-year attrition rates than either of the Guard components (Figure 3.16). As with the other components, first-year loss rates have declined substantially since the 1980s. Attrition rates among junior personnel have fallen from 37

---

[6]It is possible that because of the large pool of Navy losses, the NR is showing selectivity in retaining its new gains. However, the large attrition rate does impose costs in terms of recruiting, training (or retraining), and eventually readiness of units.

[7]As we mentioned above, most new prior-service affiliations are in a Reserve Component associated with the individual's active-duty service. As a result, first-year attrition in the ARNG and NR, for example, reflects losses of individuals with active-duty experience in the active Army and Navy. Many Marine Corps personnel do affiliate with the ARNG and the USAR, but these gains constitute a small share in these components. The attrition trends for Marine Corps personnel affiliating with the ARNG and USAR are similar to that of Army members joining these units.

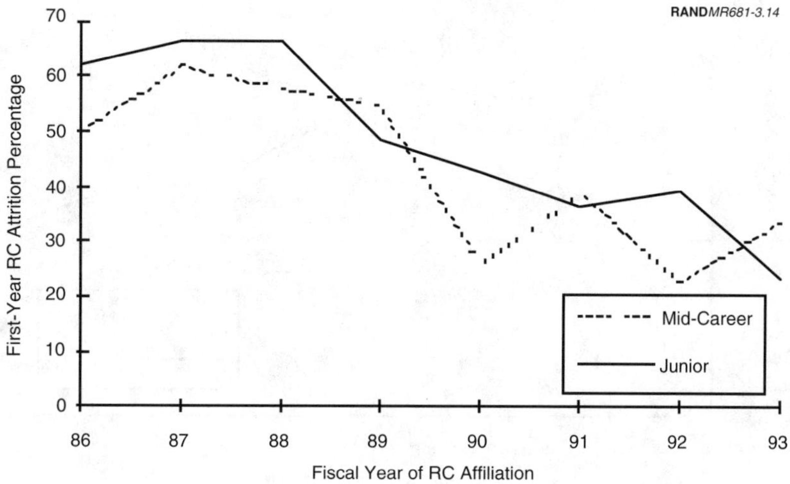

Figure 3.14—Trends in First-Year Attrition Rates of New Prior-Service Gains to the MCR, FY86–FY93

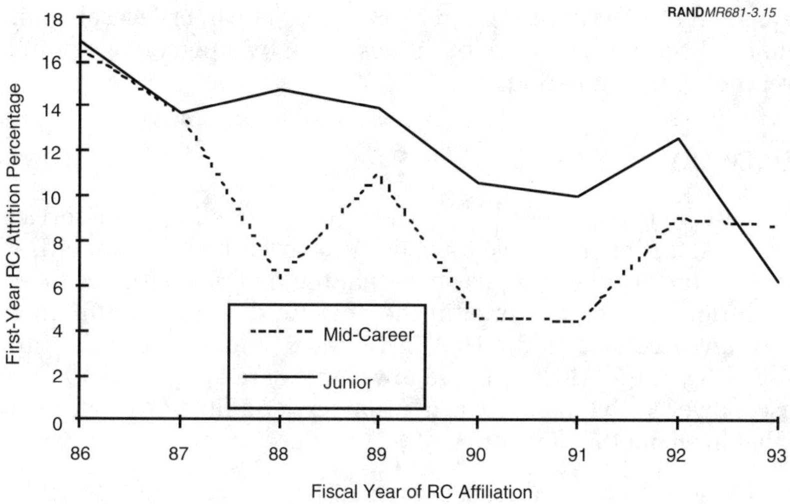

Figure 3.15—Trends in First-Year Attrition Rates of New Prior-Service Gains to the ANG, FY86–FY93

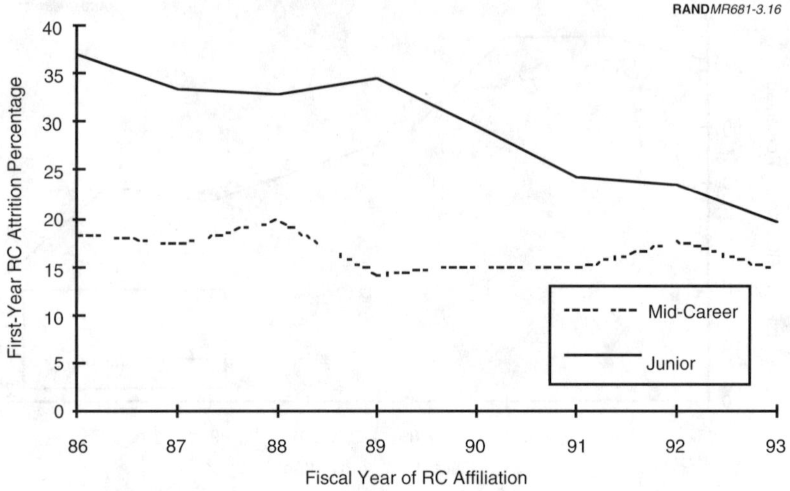

Figure 3.16—Trends in First-Year Attrition Rates of New Prior-Service Gains to the AFR, FY86–FY93

percent in FY86 to 19 percent in FY93. The mid-career-level attrition rate has been rather stable, but it has fallen by 3 percentage points over the eight-year period.

SUMMARY

The Reserve Components are doing well in attracting prior-service personnel during the active force drawdown. Table 3.3 summarizes this chapter. The early signs show that the reserve continues to attract prior-service personnel in the post–Cold War era. Affiliation rates have declined in the USAR, NR, MCR, and AFR, but they are improving in the ARNG. These lower rates are applied to a larger base, however, so the numbers of prior-service affiliations have been higher in all but the AFR and ANG.

The reserves have improved the use of prior-service personnel by improving the job match of new members. The job match rates have increased in all components but the USAR. The match rate in the USAR has been stable, but the USAR has sustained a relatively high match rate while absorbing large numbers of new prior-service gains during the active Army drawdown.

All components are doing a better job of retaining these new prior-service gains. Reserve attrition has declined, so the reserves are getting more service from recent prior-service gains than from those of the Cold War era.

Table 3.3

Summary of New Prior-Service Gains

Selected Reserve Component	Affiliation Rate	Affiliation Numbers	Job Match	Reserve Attrition
ARNG	Better	Better	Better	Better
USAR	Worse	Better	Stable	Better
NR	Worse	Better	Better	Better
MCR	Worse	Better	Better	Better
ANG	Stable	Stable	Better	Better
AFR	Worse	Stable	Better	Better

Chapter Four

ATTRITION IN THE SELECTED RESERVE COMPONENTS

As we pointed out in the last chapter, attrition of trained personnel from the reserve is costly in terms of both the high recruiting and training costs it imposes (in addition to the loss of training investment in the individual) and its detrimental effect on unit readiness. Attrition has traditionally counted all separations from a component, as was done in the last chapter; this provides the highest measure of losses. However, as Kirby and Grissmer (1993) showed, it is important to track losses forward because many Selected reservists return to the Selected Reserve or, in some cases, to the active force. Among FY82–FY86 nonprior-service gains, for example, the analysis found that only one-third to one-half of all losses were to civilian life. Some joined the active force; others either returned to the same component or joined another Selected Reserve Component. From a total force perspective, these individuals should not be considered "losses"; those who rejoin the reserve provide some return on their training investment and bring needed skills to the new unit or new component; those who join the active force may arguably be providing an even greater return on the original training. Indeed, in these cases, the reserve is providing a valuable screening function for the active forces and acting as a recruiting mechanism for them. It is important when analyzing attrition, therefore, to distinguish among these various types of attrition. Unfortunately, our data do not allow us to track reservists who leave to join the active force; however, we are able to track reservists forward in time to see whether and when they rejoin the Selected Reserve.

In this report, we focus mainly on the component's perspective, counting all separations from the component in calculating the attrition rate. We examine a similar set of questions for both the inventory as a whole and for gains separately. Specifically, these are:

1. Has the attrition rate changed over time? In particular, has attrition been significantly affected by Operation Desert Shield/Storm?
2. Are there differences in attrition among NPS, PS, and prior reserve service personnel? Have these differences remained stable over time?
3. What are the differences in attrition by years of service? What does this imply for the shaping of the force?
4. How does attrition differ by component? Has this pattern changed over time?

For some analyses, we disaggregate these separations into those who later rejoin the Reserve Components and those who appear to be permanent reserve losses (in the latter measure, those who return later to the Reserve Components are not counted as losses).

INVENTORY ATTRITION

Inventory attrition is the major determinant, along with end-strengths, of the demand for replacement reservists. It provides an aggregated rate of turnover from the reserves. Our main focus is on FY89–FY93 inventories. We were able to follow each group forward for at least a year. For the two-year comparisons, we used FY89 and FY92 inventories because we did not observe the FY93 inventory for more than one year. For each inventory, we compared the status of individuals in the inventory at the end of one year and two years to see if they were still serving in the component and were part of the Selected Reserve strength. If they were not (regardless of whether they were in another Selected Reserve Component), they were counted as losses. Thus, individuals who joined another component, the Individual Ready Reserve, or who left for civilian life were all counted in the numerator when calculating the attrition rate.

Differences in Attrition by Type of Personnel and Experience

We first look at differences in attrition among the two types of personnel: no prior active service—which includes nonprior-service personnel (i.e., those with *no prior* military service, whether active or reserve, referred to as NPS gains) and those with prior reserve service—and prior active service (PS). Annual attrition for the inventory as a whole has remained remarkably stable—a little over 21 percent left the reserve in both FY89 and FY93. As Figure 4.1 shows, the attrition rate is quite similar over all types of personnel: 20–22 percent. The low rates shown for FY90 (measured by the proportions of reservists separating during FY91) are the result of the stoploss order that was promulgated in the wake of ODS/S. This also explains the increase (to levels before the stoploss order) in the subsequent year. However, apart from this anomaly, the attrition rates have remained remarkably stable over time. Contrary to gloomy predictions, ODS/S does not appear to have resulted in a huge outflow of reservists in the succeeding years. The slight rise in inventory attrition for the later-year inventories could be the result of the drawdown as units were reorganized or closed down.

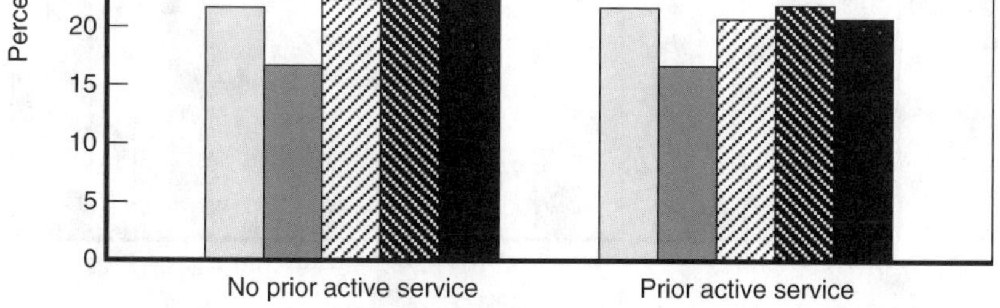

Figure 4.1—Annual Inventory Attrition Rates by Type of Personnel, FY89–FY93

The distribution of attrition rates by years of service is shown in Figure 4.2. The pattern reveals the expected U-shaped relationship between attrition rates and years of service: Reservists in their mid-career, with 10–24 years of service, tend to have very low attrition rates—8–15 percent—partly because of self-selection and partly because of vesting in the retirement system; those at the low and high ends of the distribution have attrition rates that are considerably higher, on the order of 25–30 percent. Comparing FY89 to FY93 inventory attrition rates, we see small changes in the pattern of attrition: It is slightly lower for the more junior personnel and somewhat higher for those with 6–20 years of service. The latter may be due to the drawdown and the separation benefits that are being offered to mid-career reservists. The fact that early attrition among those with fewer than six years of service is lower for the FY93 inventory offers some good news to the reserve, where early, unprogrammed attrition has always been a serious problem.

Figure 4.3 shows the attrition rates for prior-service enlisted personnel by years of *active* service. Surprisingly, there appears to be little difference in the annual attrition rates, regardless of the active-duty

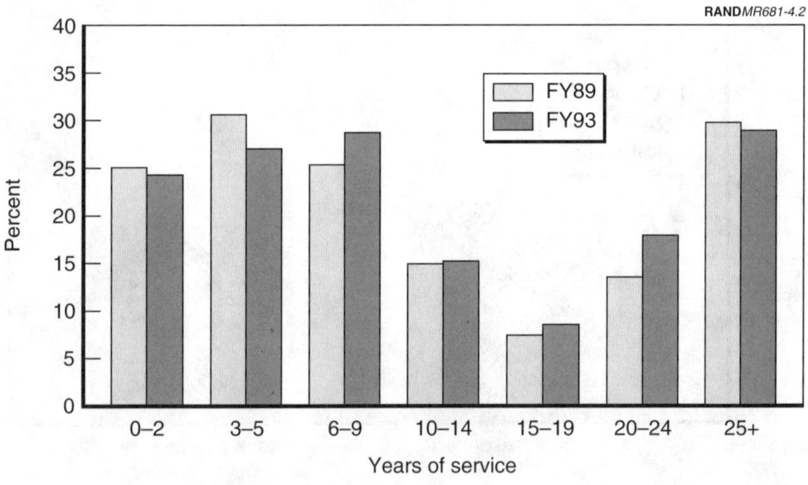

Figure 4.2—Annual Inventory Attrition Rates by Years of Service, FY89 and FY93

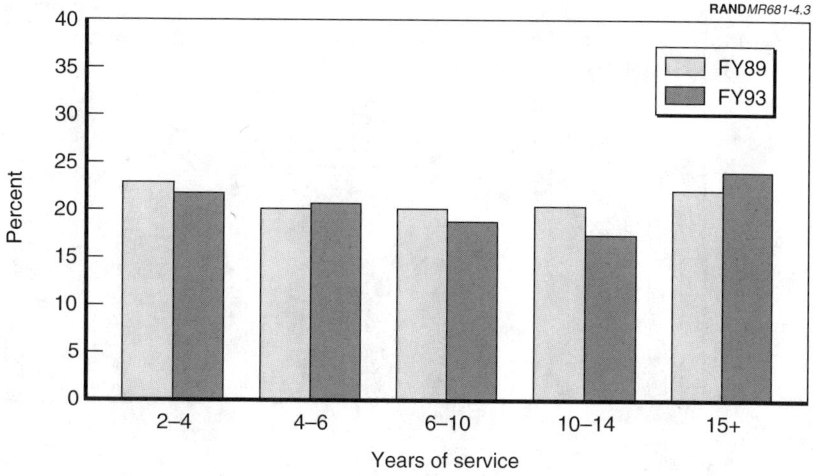

Figure 4.3—Annual Inventory Attrition Rates of Prior Active Service Personnel by Years of Active Service, FY89 and FY93

experience of the individual. On average, 20–22 percent of PS individuals leave the reserve every year, regardless of how senior they are or how much experience they brought with them into the reserve. It is interesting to note that the rates appear to have fallen slightly over time.

Differences in Attrition by Component

There are large differences in attrition rates across components, as shown in Figure 4.4, but the patterns are very similar for the two types of personnel. Regardless of type of personnel, the lowest attrition rates are among the two Air Reserve Components, where annual attrition is between 10 and 15 percent. The ARNG has an overall attrition rate of 21 percent and this has fallen to 19 percent for the FY93 inventory.

The USAR, NR, and MCR experience loss rates from inventory of 22–30 percent.

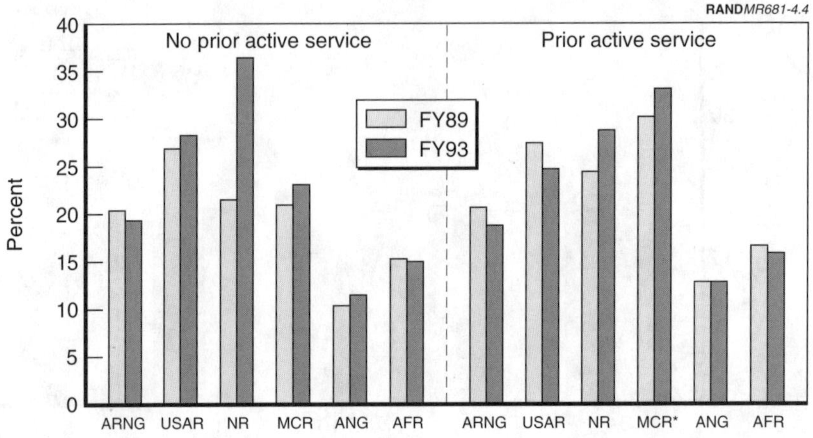

*Small sample size.

Figure 4.4—Annual Inventory Attrition Rates by Reserve Component and Type of Personnel, FY89 and FY93

The inventory loss rate has increased modestly in almost every component (and markedly in the NR) for FY93 reservists without prior active service. In the NR and MCR, PS reservists also show an increase in attrition over time, unlike the other components which show a slight decline in the attrition rate. The NR increase may be triggered by the large naval reserve drawdown.

ATTRITION RATES OF GAIN COHORTS

We turn now to attrition of the gain cohorts. It is important to distinguish their attrition behavior from that of the inventory because it may be driven by very different factors and will probably be a better predictor of what attrition is likely to be in the near future. New entrants to the reserve force are reacting to the immediate environment and reflecting the effects of recent policies, whereas the inventory may be dominated by the behavior of self-selected individuals (i.e., those who have chosen to stay in the reserve at various separation points) with strong ties to the reserve and strong ties to the retirement system.

Kirby and Grissmer (1993) point to the importance of defining a policy perspective first when defining attrition. From a component's point of view, all separations are losses because they impose costs for recruiting and training and because they have an effect on readiness of the units. However, from the perspective of the Selected Reserve, transfers and returns to another component (or later to the same component) impose lower costs than those who leave for civilian life or for active service and considerably lower costs if these reservists can use their previous skills in the new component/position.

To distinguish between these two perspectives, we calculate two variables measuring time in service:

- *Continuous time in the component,* which counts all quarters of service in the same component starting from the quarter in which personnel were gained. Thus, we measure attrition from the component's perspective and treat all transfers as attrition.
- *Total time in the reserve,* which counts all quarters of service, regardless of whether the time was served in the same component or interrupted by a separation. For those still serving at the end of FY94 (the last quarter for which we have data), this measure is not entirely accurate because it does not fully reflect how long personnel will continue to serve (usually referred to as censored observations). Despite that, it offers a useful and, from the perspective of the Selected Reserve as a whole, a more realistic measure of total time served.

For this analysis, we distinguish among NPS accessions, who enter without *any* prior military experience, prior reserve service accessions, and prior active service accessions.

One-year and two-year attrition statistics are calculated from these two variables by examining who leaves within one or two years after joining. Thus, attrition statistics are based on actual quarter joined and time thereafter regardless of when the individual joins; this method of calculating attrition provides a more accurate measure of attrition.[1] Reservists who have been in the component for less than a year (or for two years, depending on the attrition measure) and who have not yet separated as of the end of the time period in question are not counted as part of the denominator.

Figures 4.5 and 4.6 show one-year and two-year attrition rates for the different types of personnel for the FY89–FY93 accession cohorts. Approximately 20 percent of those without prior military experience (NPS gains) leave within one year of joining. The comparable attrition rate for prior-service gains, both reserve and active, is considerably higher—30–35 percent. However, a distinction should be made between early NPS attrition—attrition before the end of the enlisted term of service (ETS)—and prior-service attrition rates, which reflect separations after the usual one-year commitment term is completed.

Overall, there appears to be a small increase in attrition over time among the later cohorts of NPS gains, and there is quite a marked increase in the one-year attrition rate of prior reserve service gains. The increase may be due to an increase in involuntary attrition

RAND*MR681-4.5*

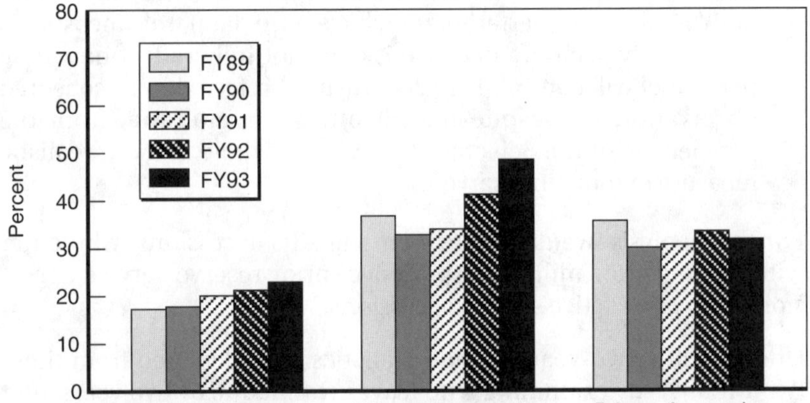

Figure 4.5—One-Year Attrition Rate by Type of Gain, FY89–FY93

[1] Grouping reservists by fiscal years, as we did with the inventory statistics, and examining who left by the end of the next fiscal year is a little misleading—not everybody in the file has had exactly the same period of time in which to separate or not.

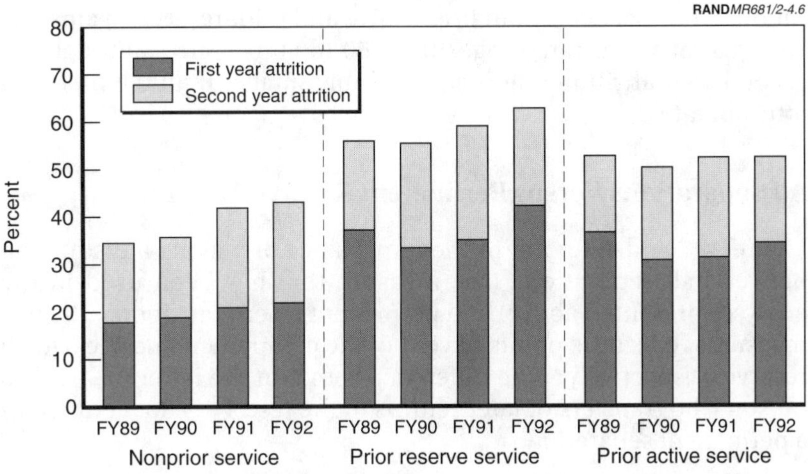

Figure 4.6—Two-Year Attrition Rate by Type of Gain, FY89–FY93

caused by the downsizing of the Reserve Components or it may be voluntary attrition because of a change in attitude regarding military service. However, the increase does not appear to have affected prior active service gains, among whom attrition remained essentially constant at about 31–32 percent. This difference in pattern could be partially explained if Reserve Components were emphasizing recruiting and retaining PS gains. On the whole, ODS/S does not appear to have triggered any large effect on attrition behavior.

The rate at which NPS gains leave during the second year is almost equal to their first-year attrition rate.[2] Overall, about 40 percent of NPS gains are lost by the end of the second year—a rather large turnover, which means an increase in recruiting costs and a loss of the early investment in training these recruits. However, as we show in the next section, some of these reservists later return and the actual loss to the Reserve Components is generally lower than the rates shown above.

---

[2]Again, for the FY92 accession cohort, only those joining in the first two quarters are being counted in the second-year rate.

Among prior-service—both prior active and prior reserve—gains, the two-year attrition rate ranges from 50 to 60 percent, although the second-year attrition rate is considerably smaller than the first-year attrition rate.

All Separations Versus Permanent Reserve Attrition

Figures 4.7 and 4.8 point to the importance of making a distinction between all separations (the measure that has been used in the analyses presented above) and permanent reserve attrition. The two measures reflect the points of view of the component and the overall reserve, respectively. The difference is that in the latter measure, a person who transfers or later returns to the reserve is not counted as a permanent separation.

Looking first at FY89, we find that 16 to 20 percent of those leaving in the first or second year later return to the Reserve Component, so that permanent reserve attrition is 80–84 percent of all losses.[3] Among the FY92–FY93 cohorts, reservists have had a much shorter time—a year for the FY93 cohort and two years for the FY92 cohort—over which to return, compared to the FY89 cohort, for whom we have a four-and-a-half-year history. Thus, because our data are limited in time, this censoring leads to an underestimate of those who will eventually return to the reserve, and the permanent reserve attrition rates for the later cohorts are likely to be overstated. The pattern, however, is still the same—permanent attrition is about 3–6 percentage points lower than the overall attrition rate. In addition, permanent attrition rates also mirror the same increase for the later cohorts of those without prior active service (NPS and prior reserve service) that we found with the overall separation rates. For example, permanent attrition rates were 14 percent for FY89 NPS gains and this had increased to 20–21 percent for the FY92–FY93 gains. Similarly, prior reserve service permanent attrition rates showed a

---

[3]Earlier work has found that a significant number of NPS gains join the active force; many apparently use the reserve as a testing ground for their compatibility with military life. Our data, however, do not allow us to distinguish these reservists from those leaving for civilian life. Thus, from the total force perspective, actual losses of NPS gains could be even smaller (Kirby and Grissmer, 1993).

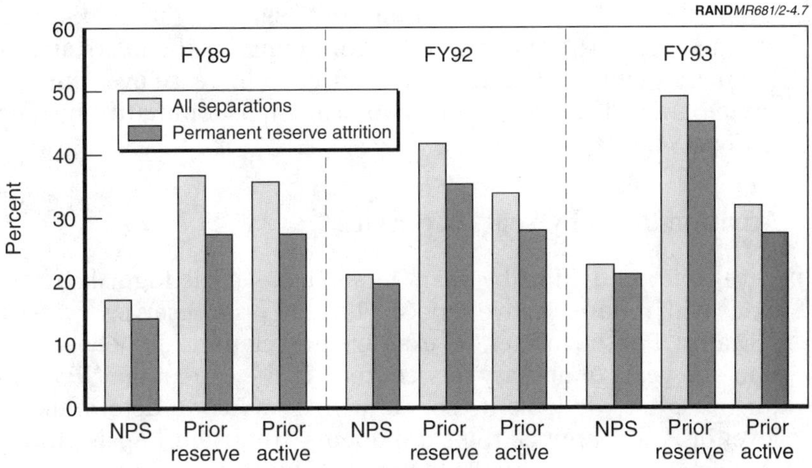

Figure 4.7—One-Year Snapshot: All Separations Versus Permanent Reserve Attrition by Type of Gain, FY89, FY92, and FY93

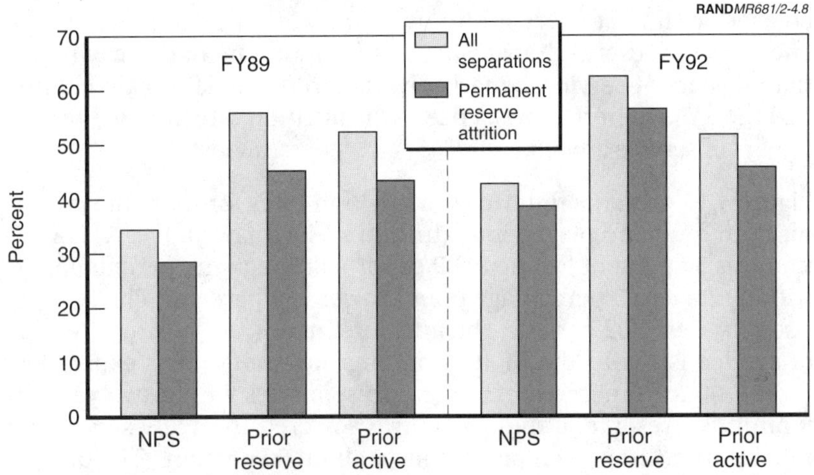

Figure 4.8—Two-Year Snapshot: All Separations Versus Permanent Reserve Attrition by Type of Gain, FY89 and FY92

large increase from 28 percent for the FY89 cohort to 35–45 percent for the FY92–FY93 cohorts. Even correcting for the overstatement, the permanent attrition rates still reflect an increase over time. The same pattern is evident in the two-year snapshot of attrition shown in Figure 4.8.

Attrition Rates by Years of Service

To examine attrition by years of service, we distinguish between gains with no prior active service (NPS and prior reserve service) and PS gains. For the former, we examine the relationship between attrition and years of military service (zero, in the case of the NPS gains); for the latter, we look at years of active service to determine what level of PS experience the components are losing. Again, through this analysis, we maintain the distinction between permanent reserve attrition and all separations.

Figure 4.9 shows the one-year attrition rate for the FY89, FY92, and FY93 gain cohorts disaggregated by years of prior service. Here we focus on those without any prior active service. Attrition has increased in almost every group over time, and this may reflect the effects of the reserve drawdown. The attrition rate of those with less than 6 years of service is markedly higher for the later gain cohorts and the FY93 cohort shows a rise in the attrition rate of those with 6–9 years of service as well.

Figure 4.10 presents the two-year attrition rates for the same groups for both total and permanent attrition. As we saw above, NPS attrition was 34 percent for the FY89 cohort, although the permanent attrition rate was 5 percentage points lower: 29 percent. The rate has risen for the FY92 cohort. The attrition rate for those with 3–5 years of service is by far the highest among the rates across experience levels: 60 to 70 percent of this group separates within two years of joining the reserve, although returns lowered the FY89 separation rate by about 10 percentage points to about 50 percent. The permanent attrition rates for the more experienced reservists are lower, about 45 percent for those with 6 or more years of service. However, it is interesting to note that the attrition rate for those with 10 or more years of service is much smaller for the FY92 cohort compared to that of the FY89 cohort (a difference in permanent attrition of over

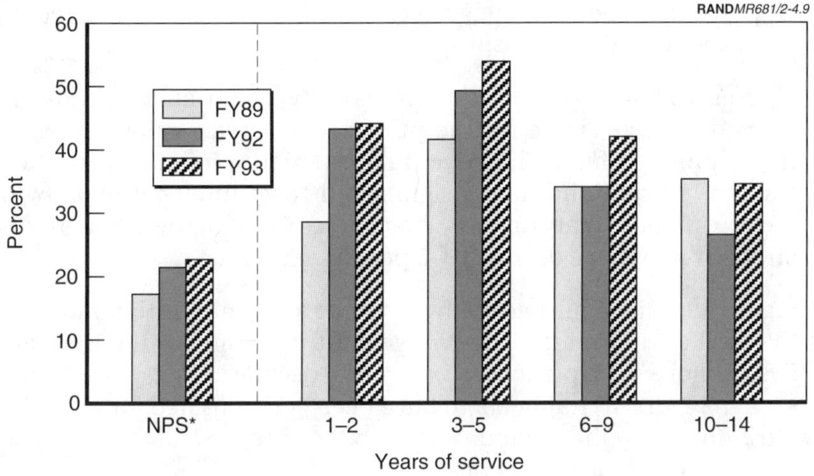

*No prior military experience—active or reserve.

Figure 4.9—One-Year Attrition Rate of Gains with No Prior Active Service by Years of Service, FY89, FY92, and FY93

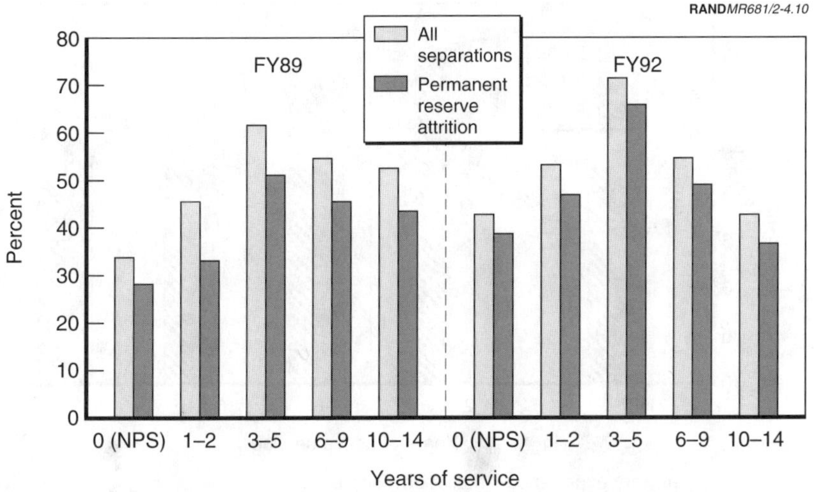

Figure 4.10—Two-Year Snapshot: All Separations Versus Permanent Reserve Attrition of Gains with No Prior Active Service by Years of Service, FY89 and FY92

10 percentage points), suggesting that the downsizing is affecting less-experienced gains disproportionately.

Figures 4.11–4.12 present the one- and two-year attrition rates by years of active service for the prior active service gains. Attrition rates appear to fall with active-duty experience in an almost linear fashion. Attrition has fallen significantly over time, particularly for those with more than 10 years of active service. For the other groups, one-year rates have declined 3–5 percentage points.

Figure 4.12 distinguishes the two-year permanent attrition rate from the total attrition rate. The two-year attrition rate for the FY89 and FY92 cohorts is surprisingly similar—the decline in first-year attrition seen in Figure 4.11 appears to have been compensated for by higher attrition during the second year, with the exception of those with 10 or more years of active service.

Not surprisingly, the permanent attrition rate for those with 10 or more years of active service is much lower than for those gains with less than 10 years of service: 32 percent compared to 40–45 percent.

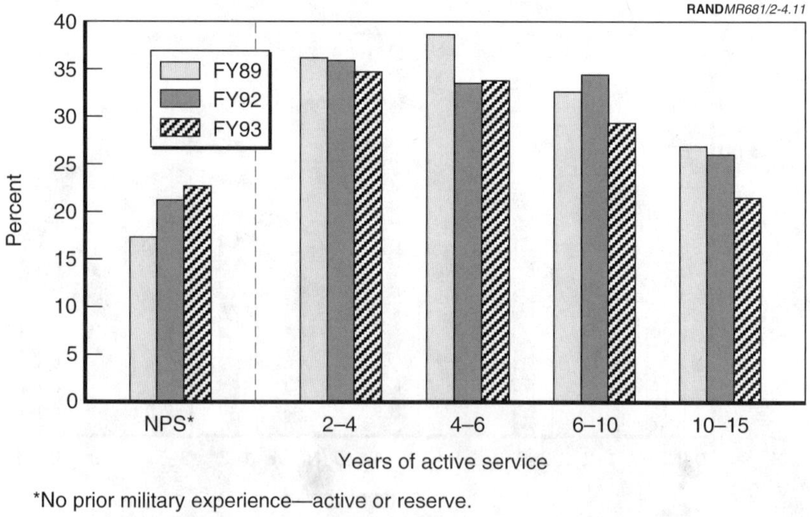

Figure 4.11—One-Year Attrition Rate of Gains with Prior Active Service by Years of Active Service, FY89, FY92, and FY93

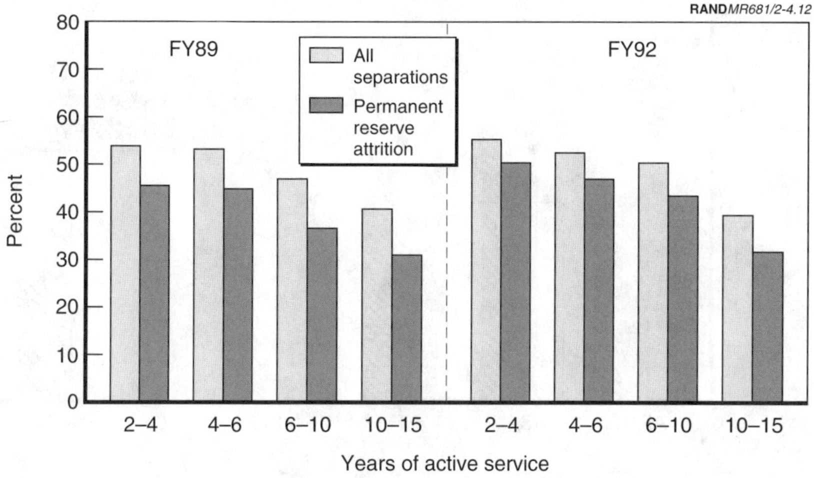

Figure 4.12—All Separations Versus Permanent Reserve Attrition of Gains with Prior Active Service by Years of Active Service, FY89 and FY92

Patterns of Attrition Among the Reserve Components: NPS Gains

Differences in attrition among the Reserve Components are seen most clearly when we examine NPS gains, because these reservists are all starting out with no military experience. Earlier work has shown that attrition differs markedly across the Reserve Components (Kirby and Grissmer, 1993), and this is clearly seen in Figures 4.13–4.14, which present the one-year and two-year attrition rates for NPS gain cohorts over time. The first-year attrition rates show some instability, although the general trend appears to be higher attrition for the later cohorts. Attrition is highest in the USAR (55 percent for FY92 gains), followed by the ARNG (39 percent), and lowest in the ANG and MCR (20 percent). The two remaining components have attrition rates of 31 (AFR) and 37 percent (NR). A second point to note is that with the exception of the MCR, where attrition actually declined slightly, there has been an increase in attrition—of about 5-10 percentage points—for the FY92–FY93 NPS gain cohorts compared with that of the FY89 cohort. This increase may be partly due to tightening of training standards or "creaming" of the gain

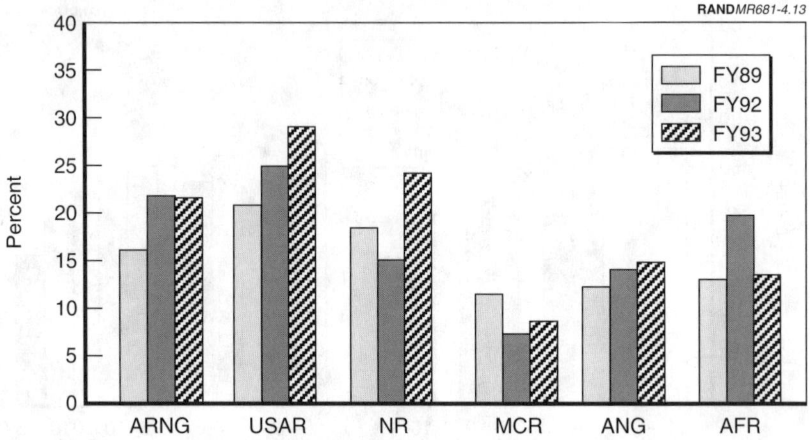

Figure 4.13—One-Year Attrition Rate of Nonprior-Service Enlisted Gains by Reserve Component, FY89, FY92, and FY93

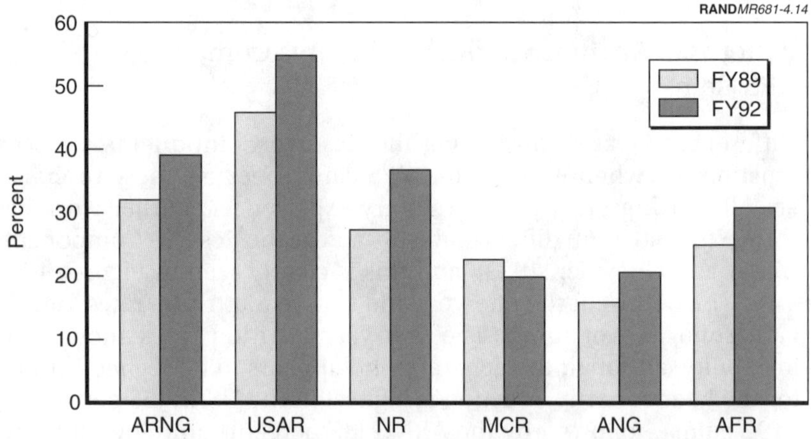

Figure 4.14—Two-Year Attrition Rate of Nonprior-Service Enlisted Gains by Reserve Component, FY89 and FY92

cohorts in response to the need to reduce the overall size of the Reserve Components.

Figure 4.15 distinguishes all separations from permanent reserve separation for the components. For the FY89 gain cohort, returns to the Selected Reserve lowered the overall separation rate by about 3–9 percentage points. The highest proportion of returns (almost 20 percent of those separating) was among the Army Reserve gains, who also had the highest rate of attrition. The returnees lowered the permanent attrition rate to 37 percent from 46 percent. Returns for the FY92 cohort are much lower—not surprising, given our censored data. However, it is difficult to predict whether the permanent attrition rate will actually be much lower than the range shown, because downsizing may well limit returns and transfers.

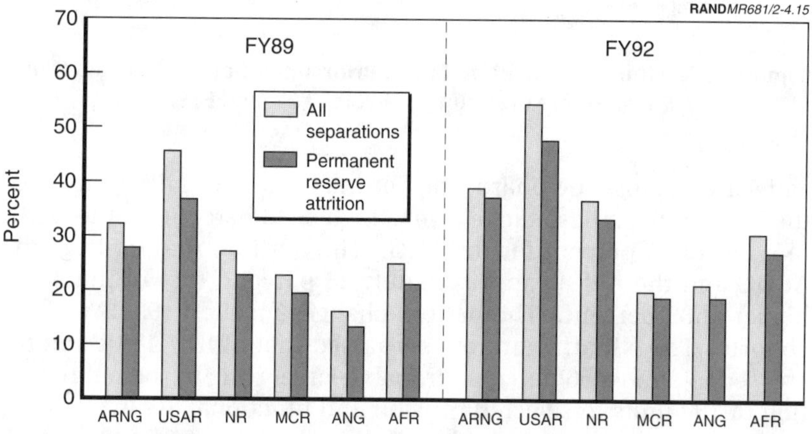

Figure 4.15—Two-Year Snapshot: All Separations Versus Permanent Reserve Attrition of Nonprior-Service Enlisted Gains by Reserve Component, FY89 and FY92

Patterns of Attrition Among the Reserve Components: PS Gains

The attrition behavior of PS gains across the Reserve Components determines, among other factors, the differences in PS content of the Reserve Components. As Figure 4.16 shows, attrition rates for PS

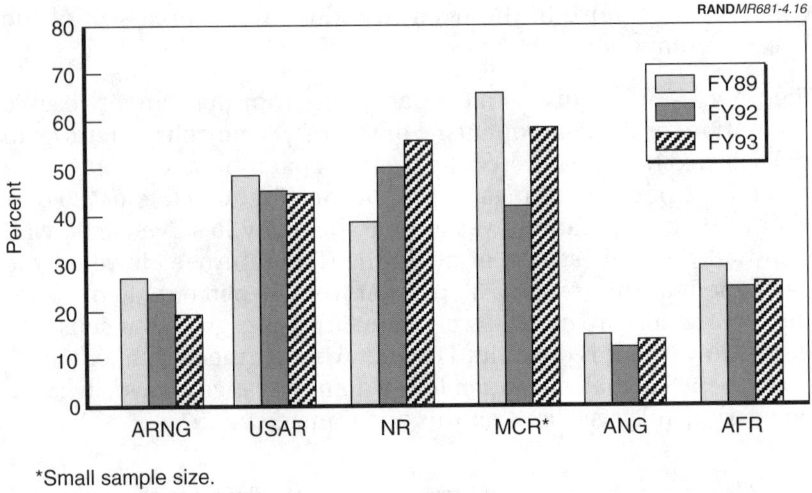

Figure 4.16—One-Year Attrition Rate of Prior Active Service Enlisted Gains by Reserve Component, FY89, FY92, and FY93

gains are—across the board—higher than those for NPS gains. For the FY89 cohort, these range from a high of 49 percent for the USAR to a low of 15 percent for the ANG. The attrition rate for both the ARNG and the AFR is approximately 28 percent; that of the NR is higher at 39 percent. The pattern changes for the FY92–FY93 gain cohorts. The NR attrition rate surpassed that of the USAR and increased to almost 56 percent, probably largely due to the net reduction of 100 units in selected mission and functional areas.[4] For the remaining components, attrition declined by 1–8 percent. Two-year attrition rates follow the same pattern (Figure 4.17), although the decline is not quite as marked.

Figure 4.18 breaks out all losses from permanent reserve attrition. About 20 percent of those leaving the Air Reserve Components later

[4]These included reductions in mission areas (such as control of shipping, communications, and intelligence) and functional areas (such as ship augmentation and base and staff support).

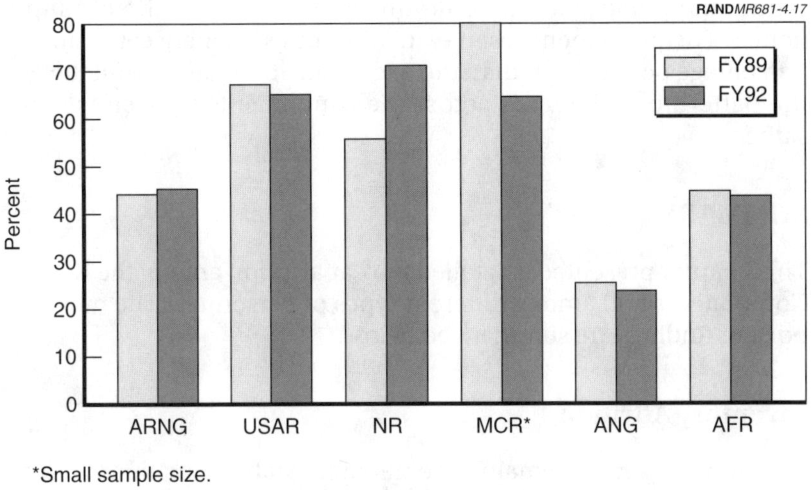

Figure 4.17—Two-Year Attrition Rate of Prior Active Service Enlisted Gains by Reserve Component, FY89 and FY92

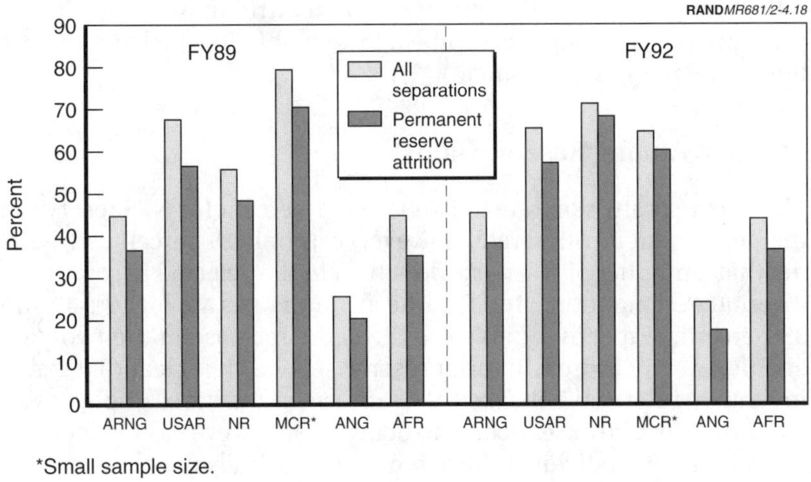

Figure 4.18—Two-Year Snapshot: All Separations Versus Permanent Reserve Attrition of Prior Active Service Enlisted Gains by Reserve Component, FY89 and FY92

return; the proportions are little smaller for the other three components. The permanent reserve attrition rates are between 5 and 10 percentage points lower than the overall attrition rates. Nonetheless, the pattern of differences across the components is essentially the same.

SUMMARY

This chapter presented a detailed look at attrition among the Reserve Components and among different types of personnel. The most important findings are summarized below.

Inventory Attrition

Attrition rates have remained remarkably stable over time. A little over 21 percent leave the force each year and this attrition rate is quite similar over all types of personnel—those with prior active service and those without prior active service. There are large differences in attrition rates across components: The Air Reserve Components have the lowest attrition rates; 10–15 percent; the others range from 21–30 percent. Annual attrition of those without prior active service appears to be a little higher for the later cohorts but the increase is quite small.

Attrition Among Reserve Gains

The two-year attrition rate in FY89 was 34 percent for NPS reservists; the permanent attrition rate, however, was only 29 percent, suggesting that a number of reservists do return to the Selected Reserve after a period of separation. By FY92, the attrition rates are higher: 42 and 39 percent, respectively. We see the same increase in the two-year attrition rate of those with prior reserve service. It is clear that stable inventory rates have masked the upturn in attrition among gains without prior active service. Balancing this, however, is the fact that the rates for PS individuals have remained basically unchanged.

Table 4.1 summarizes the recent attrition experience of the Reserve Components for both the inventory as a whole and for gains.

This chapter examined attrition largely from the component perspective. What eventually determines the overall readiness of the component is what occurs at the unit level. The next chapter examines turbulence and skill-qualification rates at the unit level.

Table 4.1

Summary of Changes in Attrition Rates, FY89–FY93

Selected Reserve Component	NPS Inventory	PS Inventory	NPS Gains	PS Gains
ARNG	Better	Better	Worse	Stable
USAR	Worse	Better	Worse	Stable
NR	Worse	Worse	Worse	Worse
MCR	Worse	Worse	Better	Better
ANG	Worse	Stable	Worse	Stable
AFR	Stable	Better	Worse	Stable

Chapter Five

TRENDS IN SKILL QUALIFICATION AND TURBULENCE

The readiness of Selected Reserve units is degraded if members are not skill-qualified in their assigned jobs. At mobilization, in many cases, these personnel may need to be trained or replaced with qualified personnel before the unit is ready for deployment.[1] Both "fixes" for qualification have serious drawbacks. Retraining is time-consuming and may strain limited training-base resources. Individual training at mobilization disrupts unit preparations for deployment, since individuals involved are not available for preparatory unit exercises. Replacement disrupts unit cohesion and continuity, since replacement personnel have not trained with the unit. The replacement option is also limited by the availability of replacement personnel from other units.

Skill qualification problems are related to new members joining reserve units and existing or returning members who need retraining. New NPS members must undergo initial active-duty training (IADT). This training includes a basic training segment that concentrates on general soldiering skills and a job training segment that prepares the individual for a particular military job. New PS reservists are already proficient in a military skill and are seldom reactivated for training before joining a reserve unit. Ideally, new PS members are matched with their active-duty job, so the Selected Reserve unit benefits from the prior-service training and experience of the new member. Nonmatched PS members are retrained part-time within the unit, at

[1]In ODS/S, however, units did deploy with members who were not skill-qualified. Clearly, this is not the ideal situation.

a Reserve Component school, or occasionally during annual training periods.

The second source of skill-qualification problems is the retraining of existing members who have completed IADT. Previous studies (Buddin and Grissmer, 1994; Grissmer et al., 1994a) have shown that members frequently change jobs and need retraining. This retraining is generally very time-consuming, since reassigned reservists are seldom retrained full-time.

Some job changes are reassignments within a unit, but many changes are coincident with a change in unit. Job and unit changes reflect both individual and unit initiatives. Individuals might want a new job with better skill transferability to the civilian sector or better promotion opportunities in the reserves. Units might encourage existing members to retrain and fill a unit vacancy or might reassign or retrain existing members if unit authorizations are revised, new equipment is received (for example, units changing from M113s to Bradleys or M60 tanks to M1 tanks), or the unit itself changes from one type of unit to another. In principle, job and unit change could improve skill qualification, if members moved from positions for which they were unqualified to vacancies in their trained skill. However, these job and unit changes have historically been associated with lower skill-qualification rates.

In the remainder of this chapter, we examine trends in skill-qualification levels and job/unit turbulence. We begin by examining changes in the training pipeline of new members joining the reserves. The pipeline reflects new non-PS members who are being trained in an initial military skill. Next we examine skill-qualification problems of existing unit members. This analysis examines how job and unit turbulence affect skill qualification. Our analysis here is limited to part-time members, because they constitute the bulk of unit strength, and excludes AGR and military technicians.

THE TRAINING PIPELINE FOR THE SELECTED RESERVES

At any point in time, some share of each Reserve Component is involved in full-time, active-duty training and is unavailable to local units. These members are typically characterized as being in the training pipeline. The size of the pipeline is dictated by several factors:

- How many vacancies are available (the turnover rate),
- How many vacancies are filled by prior-service personnel (the PS content of new accessions), and
- How long it takes to train new personnel (IADT training time).

A component's training burden is greatly reduced if the turnover rate is low and vacancies are filled by PS personnel matched to their active-duty skills. Nonmatched PS personnel will also shorten the training pipeline, since these individuals are not counted in the pipeline. These nonmatched individuals hurt unit readiness, however, because they are not qualified in their skill.

IADT training time can also have a substantial effect on the training pipeline. In part, this reflects the component's mission and mix of skills necessary to accomplish that mission. Only a portion of necessary job skills are taught at IADT, however, so training time reflects the share of necessary skills taught in initial training and the share acquired from experience in the unit or annual training.

An important factor affecting the training pipeline is not the training time per se but rather the timing of training. In some cases, the pipeline is lengthened, because individual members are waiting for individual training. Some members have long training periods, because their training is split. Under split training, basic and skill training are not completed back-to-back. Rather, the member is activated for basic training, returns to the local unit, and later is reactivated for skill training. Delayed and split training may be necessary because the component cannot arrange training at the appropriate times. Some potential new members might have scheduling conflicts with an employer or school and be unable to leave immediately for training or to train continuously for both basic and skill training. If other personnel are unavailable, components use training delays and split training to accommodate individuals with scheduling conflicts.

Figure 5.1 shows differences in the relative size of the training pipeline across components and how the pipeline has changed over

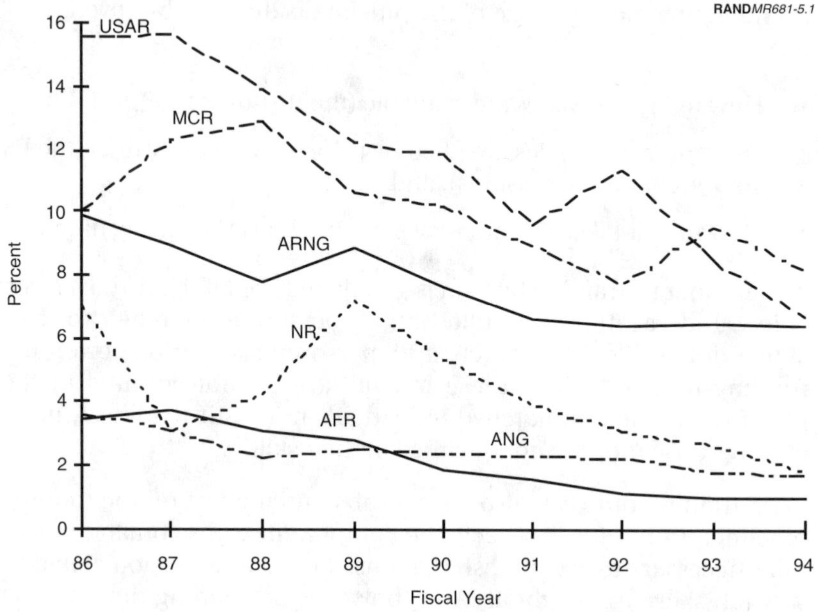

Figure 5.1—Percentage of Total Selected Reserve in Training Pipeline by Reserve Component, FY86–FY94

time. As we said above, the pipeline reflects essentially the new non-PS accessions of the component. All components have reduced the size of the training pipeline relative to that in the Cold War period. The smaller pipeline reflects improvements in PS content and reduced attrition. The reserve drawdown has also meant that reserve accession missions have been smaller than in the late 1980s, so the reserves have had reduced non-PS missions.

Both Army components have had dramatic reductions in their training pipeline. The USAR had a much larger pipeline than the other components in FY86, but the pipeline has fallen by FY94, as has the ARNG pipeline. The substantial gap between the size of the pipeline in the USAR and that in the ARNG has closed consistently over time.

Large active Army losses and reductions in ARNG and USAR end-strengths have been important factors in reducing the training pipeline for these components. As we saw above, the Army Reserve Components have been successful in attracting PS personnel from the active force drawdown. This success has been a big factor in containing the mission for new non-PS members and reducing the size of the training pipeline. As we also saw above, the USAR and to a lesser extent the ARNG have been reducing their endstrength in recent years, so they did not need many new non-PS accessions in the past few years.

Two factors suggest that this new smaller pipeline in the Army components might be difficult to sustain. First, the ARNG and USAR have traditionally had difficulty maintaining high PS content relative to other components. Second, the drawdown leaves the Army's ratio of active to reserve strength lower than before the drawdown. Unless the ARNG and USAR can attract larger shares from smaller cohorts departing the active Army, the components will need to increase their non-PS missions, and, accordingly, the training pipeline.

The NR pipeline has also been reduced. The pipeline size was volatile in the Cold War period, falling from 7 percent in FY86 to 3 and 4 percent in FY87 and FY88, respectively, and then returning to 7 percent again in FY89. Since FY89, the size of the pipeline has been reduced consistently to only 2 percent in FY94. The NR has taken the largest reductions in endstrength during the reserve drawdown, so the NR has fewer vacancies and is able to fill a smaller share of its recruiting mission with new non-PS personnel.

The pipeline has also been reduced in the MCR, although its size has gone up and down somewhat erratically over time. The surprising factor in the MCR pipeline is that a component with such a large share of non-PS personnel can sustain such a small training pipeline. A major factor in this success is the ability of the MCR to fill its recruiting mission without resorting to delayed or split training options. Unlike the Army components, delayed and split training are rare in the MCR, so the training period is compressed and the pipeline is shortened.

The small training pipeline for the Air Reserve Components reflects successes in other personnel programs. The components have low turnover and high prior-service content. The pipeline size is small, because the Air Reserve Components have few vacancies and fill most of them with PS personnel. Only about 4 percent of ANG and AFR personnel were in the training pipeline in FY86, compared with 16 and 10 percent in the USAR and ARNG, respectively. Even with this small pipeline, however, the Air Reserve Components have reduced the size of the pipeline in recent years: by FY94, 2 and 1 percent of ANG and AFR personnel were in the training pipeline.

SKILL QUALIFICATION AND TURBULENCE IN THE ARNG AND USAR

The Army components have been plagued by low skill-qualification levels. In some respects, PS personnel appear to have lower skill-qualification rates than non-PS personnel, but the comparison depends on whether the training pipeline is included in the computations. Since the pipeline includes almost exclusively non-PS personnel, the qualification rates for non-PS personnel are noticeably lower across all non-PS personnel than across those non-PS personnel not in the training pipeline. Figure 5.2 shows what share of personnel are not skill-qualified for three categories: PS members, non-PS members who are not in the training pipeline, and total non-PS members (including those in and out of the pipeline).

The ARNG results show that non-PS personnel skill-qualification rates are higher than those of PS personnel, if we do not count the training pipeline, but the difference disappears when the pipeline is included. In FY86, for example, 30 percent of PS personnel were not skill-qualified as compared with 22 percent of non-PS personnel outside the pipeline, but 30 percent of the total non-PS population was unqualified. The pipeline contributes little to immediate unit readiness, so the relevant comparison of PS and non-PS personnel is the comparison of total PS and non-PS. In the ARNG, the overall rates are very similar.

The ARNG percentage of unqualified PS and non-PS personnel has fallen by about 2 or 3 percent since FY86, but the rate has been quite stable. The improvements in prior-service content, better job match rates of PS personnel, and a smaller training pipeline have done little to reduce the share of unqualified personnel in the component.

The USAR had a very large training pipeline in FY86, and this factor inflated the nonqualification rates for non-PS personnel to 45

RANDMR681-5.2

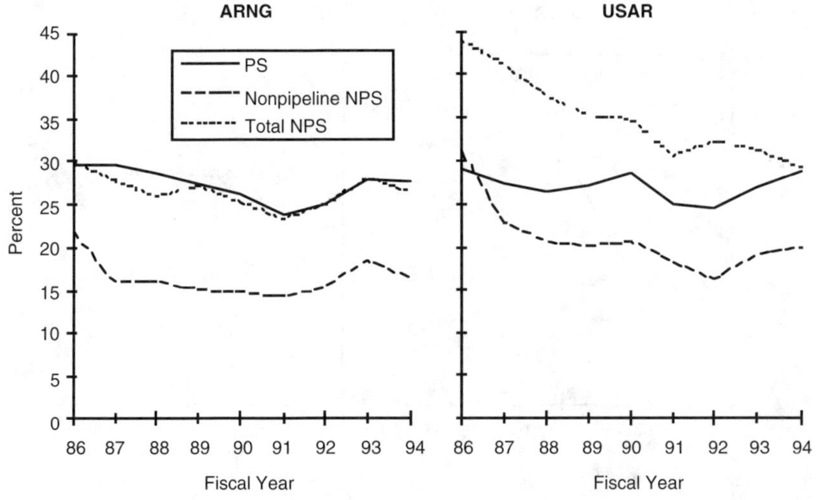

Figure 5.2—Percentage of Prior-Service and Nonprior-Service ARNG and USAR Personnel Not Skill-Qualified, FY86–FY94

percent compared with 31 percent for the those not in the pipeline. As the USAR reduced the size of the training pipeline, the nonqualification rate for non-PS members has fallen to 29 percent in FY94. The nonqualification rate of the nonpipeline group has also fallen substantially over this period, from 31 percent in FY86 to 20 percent in FY94.

Although the USAR has reduced qualification problems for non-PS personnel, PS personnel have the same rate of unqualified personnel in FY94 as in FY86—30 percent.

Why are so few unit members qualified in their assigned skill? An important part of the training burden in the reserves is the retraining of members into new jobs. Figure 5.3 shows the percentage of reservists who changed jobs or units between FY86 and FY94. The rates are computed for all PS and non-PS personnel combined, since differences by PS status were small.

In the ARNG, about 16 percent of members change jobs and unit in a year. Changing units is frequently coincident with changing jobs,

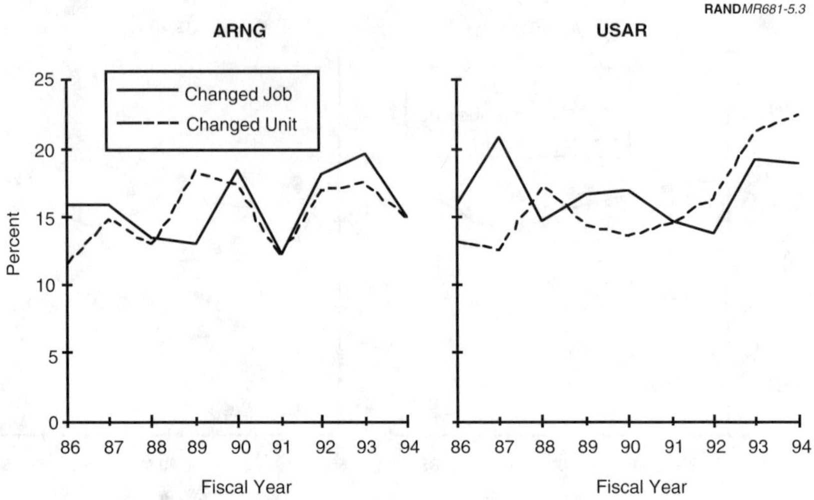

Figure 5.3—Percentage of ARNG and USAR Personnel Changing Jobs or Units in Past Year, FY86–FY94

since the new unit may not have a vacancy in the member's trained skill. The USAR rates of turbulence are also high, with unit and job change rates of 22 and 19 percent, respectively, in FY94. These turbulence rates understate the changes in unit composition itself, since the base does not include new members who enter the unit during the intervening year or those members who separate from the reserves.

Figure 5.4 shows how changes in job translate into changes in skill qualification. Most Army component members who change jobs in a year are not qualified in their new job. In the ARNG, 57 percent of job changers are unqualified as compared with only about 10 percent of members who remain in the same job. The low qualification rate of job changers shows that new skills are not acquired quickly and training times are very protracted. The much lower rates for those not changing jobs are encouraging by comparison, but the fact that 10 percent of job stayers are not qualified after another full year on the job is also indicative of long retraining times.

As in the ARNG, most USAR job changers are unqualified at their new jobs. The rate shows no strong trend, but 64 percent of job changers

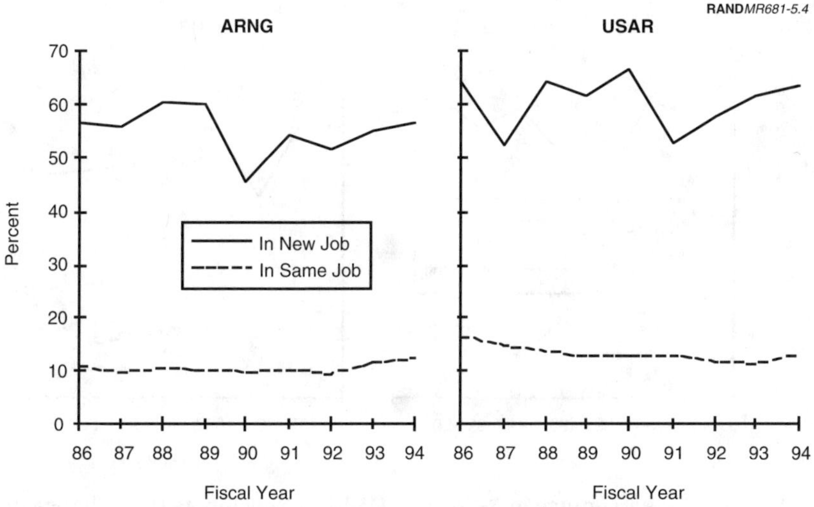

Figure 5.4—Percentage of ARNG and USAR Personnel Not Skill-Qualified by Job Change Status in Past Year, FY86–FY94

were unqualified in FY94. Among members not changing jobs, the percentage unqualified is higher in the USAR than in the ARNG, but the rate is showing some improvement—falling from 17 percent to 13 percent in the nine-year period.

Job changes are much more common among members who change units. Figure 5.5 shows that about 50 percent of ARNG members who change units also change jobs, compared with about 10 percent of those remaining in the same unit. In the USAR, the job change rate is lower for unit changers than in the ARNG, but the rate of intraunit job changes is slightly higher. The trends in percentage changing jobs do not show much movement one way or the other—the USAR job change rate in FY94 is 40 percent for those changing units compared with 13 percent for those staying in the same unit.

The inter- and intraunit levels of job change create major retraining problems for the Army components. Reassigned members are not quickly retrained in their new skill, so job turbulence is a major factor in the ARNG and USAR skill-qualification problems. Interunit competition for members is certainly a factor in this turbulence, since most members shift to a nearby unit (Buddin and Grissmer, 1994).

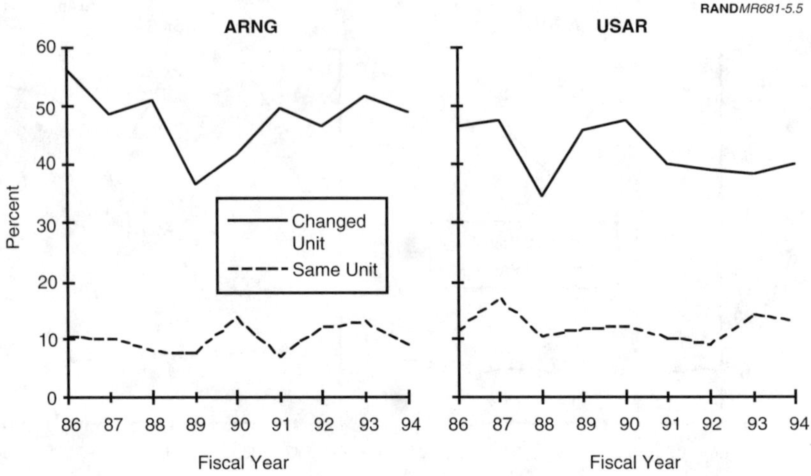

Figure 5.5—Percentage in ARNG and USAR in New Job by Unit Change in Past Year, FY86–FY94

Intraunit reassignment is also important, however. Although a smaller percentage of members change jobs within units than across units, the change rate is applied to the bigger base of members remaining with the unit. Consequently, intraunit reassignments in the Army components are a major factor affecting skill qualification.

Skill-qualification rates in the Army components have changed little over the last several years. The USAR has improved qualification rates for non-PS personnel, in part, by reducing the size of the training pipeline. Nonqualification rates remain high mainly because job and unit turbulence remain high. The frequency of job changes has not abated and job retraining (requalification) is slow.

SKILL QUALIFICATION AND TURBULENCE IN THE NR AND MCR

In the late 1980s, the NR had a much worse skill-qualification problem than the ARNG or USAR, but the share of personnel not qualified has fallen substantially in recent years. Unlike the Army components, non-PS personnel are much more likely than PS personnel to be unqualified (see Figure 5.6). Among total non-PS personnel, the

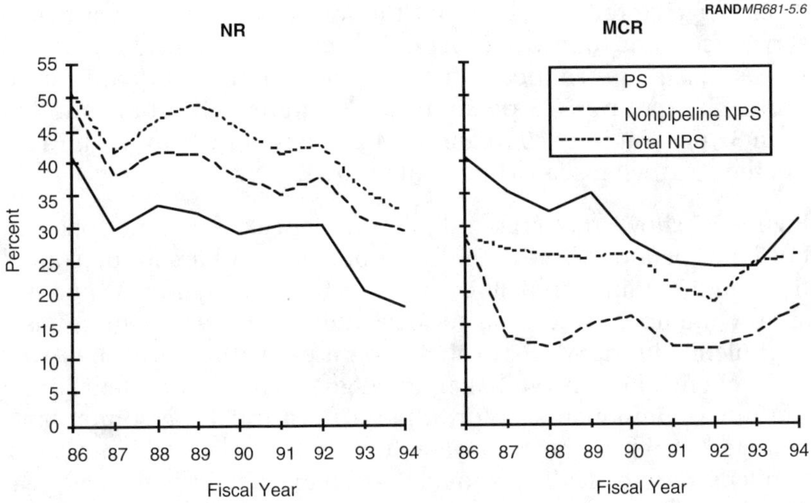

Figure 5.6—Percentage of Prior-Service and Nonprior-Service NR and MCR Personnel Not Skill-Qualified, FY86–FY94

percentage unqualified has fallen from 51 percent in FY86 to 32 percent in FY94. Even with this improvement, however, the share of non-PS unqualified remains higher than for either Army component. The NR has reduced the percentage of unqualified PS personnel from 41 to 18 percent since FY86, a substantially lower mark than the 29 percent of PS unqualified in the Army components.

The MCR has a large training pipeline of non-PS personnel, so its skill-qualification rates are quite sensitive to whether the pipeline is included in the computation of the qualification rate. Among those not in the pipeline, the non-PS nonqualification rate fell from 28 percent in FY86 to 15 percent in FY89. Since then, the rate has fallen to 11 percent in FY91 and FY92, and the nonqualification rate is 18 percent in FY94.

The share of unqualified personnel in the MCR has varied less for the total non-PS group than for the portion of the non-PS population that is not in the pipeline. The nonqualification rate fell from 29 percent in FY86 to 25 percent in FY89, but the rate has been rather stable since then. The nonqualification rate in FY94 was again 25 percent.

In earlier chapters, we saw that the MCR had much lower prior-service content than the other Reserve Components. Figure 5.6 shows that PS personnel in the MCR had more skill-qualification problems than non-PS personnel. The nonqualification rate fell from 35 percent in FY89 to about 24 percent in FY91 through FY93, but the rate then rose to 31 percent in FY94.

Figure 5.7 shows that unit and job turbulence are commonplace in both the NR and the MCR. These turbulence rates are for personnel through the training pipeline, so they reflect reassignments and not simply members returning to local units from the training base. Turbulence in the MCR is roughly on a par with that of the Army components, but the NR has much higher rates of turbulence than the other components. More than a third of NR personnel have changed units in the past year for each of the last nine years. Similarly, a third of NR personnel have changed units in the past year for all but the two most recent years.

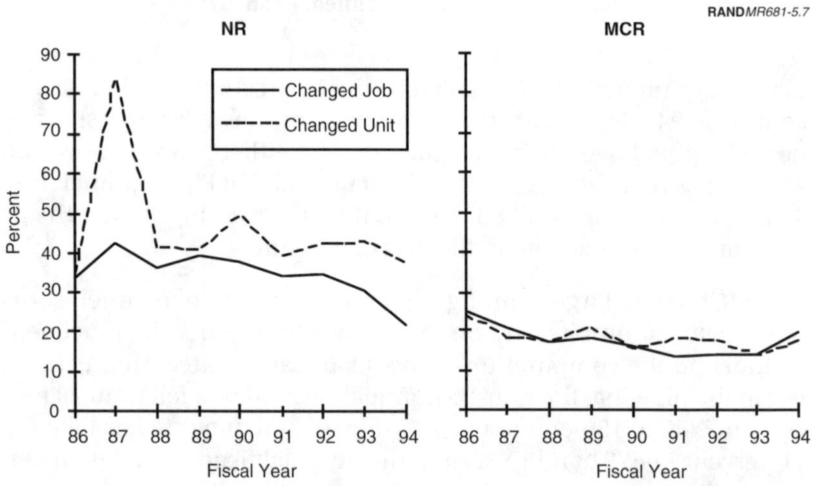

Figure 5.7—Percentage of NR and MCR Personnel Changing Jobs or Units in Past Year, FY86–FY94

The NR had an extraordinary rate of unit change between FY86 and FY87, but this change reflected institutional adjustments and not a substantial change in personnel relocations. In FY87, the NR reorganized and nearly doubled the number of units in the NR. About 84 percent of personnel were in a nominally different unit in FY87, compared with FY85. Nearly half of all NR personnel in FY87 were assigned to NR units that did not exist in FY86. In many cases, these new units were collocated with the existing units, so about 80 percent of personnel changed to a unit located within the same ZIP code area.

In the MCR, job change rates declined somewhat from 25 percent in FY86 to about 14 percent in FY91 through FY94, but the rate rose sharply to 20 percent in FY94. Rates of unit change have been more stable than rates of job change. About 18 percent of MCR personnel changed jobs in three of the past four years, and this rate of turbulence is similar to that of the late 1980s.

Job change is an important factor affecting skill qualification, because reassigned personnel are retrained slowly part-time. In the NR, the nonqualification rates for those changing jobs are much higher than for those remaining in the same job (see Figure 5.8). Even among members remaining in the same job, however, the nonqualification rate remains high after an additional year at the same job. In most years, over 20 percent of NR personnel who do not change jobs are still not qualified in their assigned skill. The nonqualification rate has fallen to 14 and 10 percent in FY93 and FY94, respectively. The slow reduction in the nonqualification rate for those remaining in the same skill is strong evidence that skill retraining is very time-consuming.

The nonqualification rate for NR personnel who changed jobs in the past year is quite high and ranges from 40–50 percent in most years.

About a third of job changers in the MCR are requalified in their new job in less than a year. In recent years, the MCR has experienced increasing delays in requalifying these reassigned members. Nonqualification rates for job changers have risen from 20 percent in FY91 to 40 percent in FY94. The MCR has lower nonqualification rates for job changers than the Army components or the NR; this

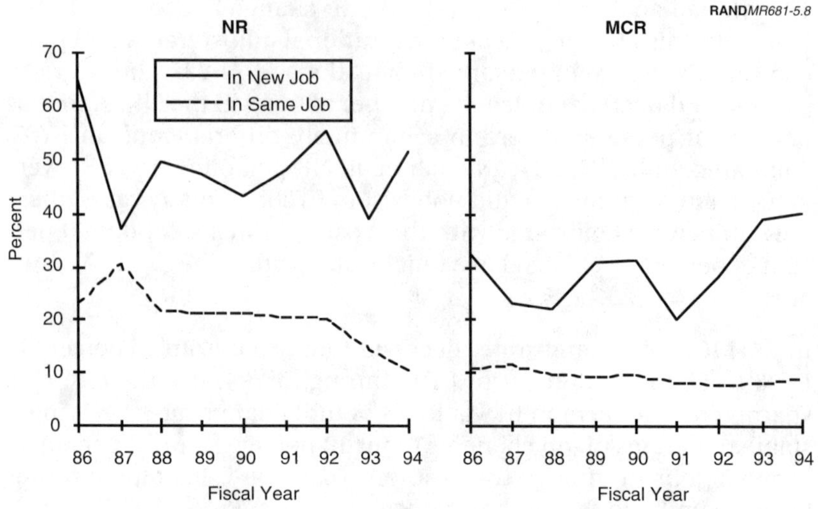

Figure 5.8—Percentage of NR and MCR Personnel Not Skill-Qualified by Job Change Status in Past Year, FY86–FY94

suggests that the MCR has shorter retraining times than these components or that the MCR is more judicious about reassigning personnel to new jobs.

Among members not changing jobs, the skill-nonqualification rates for MCR members have been low and declined a few percentage points in recent years. About 8 or 9 percent of personnel remain unqualified, however, and this suggests that the nonqualification rate is very slowly converging to zero for personnel in stable jobs.

Figure 5.9 shows that job change is much more common for NR and MCR members who change units than for those remaining in the same unit. In the NR, intraunit job change was common in FY86 and FY87, but it has fallen off substantially since then. In FY88, 16 percent of NR members changed jobs within their unit, and the rate of intraunit job change fell to only 6 percent in FY94.

Most unit changers in the NR have changed jobs as well as units. Between FY88 and FY93, about two-thirds of all interunit changes in the NR were associated with a job change. Among unit changers, job change has fallen from 69 percent in FY92 to 60 and 47 percent in

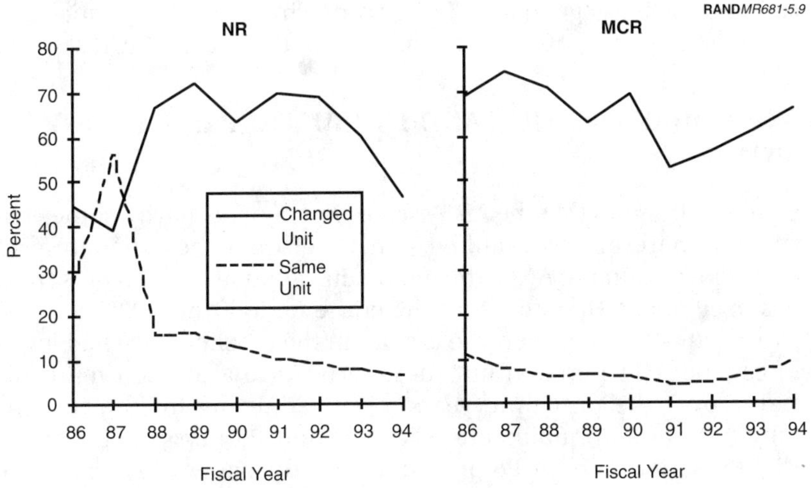

Figure 5.9—Percentage of NR and MCR Personnel in New Job by Unit Change in Past Year, FY86–FY94

FY93 and FY94, respectively. Job change is about eight times as likely for a NR member who changes units as for a member who remains in the same unit.

In the MCR, job change rates are much higher for members who change units than for members who remain in the same unit. The job change rates for unit changers and nonunit changers were 70 and 11 percent, respectively, in FY86. Job change rates declined somewhat for both unit changers and nonchangers between FY86 and FY91, but the rates have declined since then. In FY94, 66 percent of unit changers had changed jobs as compared with only 10 percent of members who remained in the same unit as the previous year.

The skill-qualification (MOSQ) and turbulence patterns for the NR and MCR are similar to those of the Army components. Skill-nonqualification rates remain high. Members frequently change jobs or units. Job change is much more likely for unit changers than for nonunit changers. Requalification at a new skill is time-consuming, so job changers have high nonqualification rates and unqualified members who do not change jobs will only slowly achieve requalification in their assigned job. The drawdown has not substantially altered the trends in MOSQ or turbulence for the NR and MCR.

SKILL QUALIFICATION AND TURBULENCE IN THE ANG AND AFR

Figure 5.10 shows that the Air Reserve Components have a somewhat smaller share of nonqualified personnel than the other Reserve Components. In the ANG, the nonqualification rate for PS personnel has been about 18 percent for the entire period from FY86 through FY94. Non-PS personnel who are not in the pipeline have had lower rates, about 11 percent, but these rates have also been markedly stable over the past nine years. After adjusting for the training pipeline, the nonqualification rate of non-PS personnel remains slightly better than for PS personnel, but the gap is only about two percentage points per year.

In the AFR, the nonqualification rates have fallen over time, but the decline occurred between FY86 and FY89, and the rates have been quite stable since then. The size of the training pipeline in the AFR has fallen to only 1 percent in recent cohorts (see Figure 5.1), so the nonqualification rate of non-PS personnel has become rather insensitive to whether the pipeline personnel are included or omitted in the computation. In FY88, the PS and total non-PS nonqualification rates were both about 17 percent. Since then, the PS rate has remained stable, and the non-PS rate has fallen to about 14 percent.

The Air Reserve Components can attribute at least part of their skill-qualification success to lower turbulence. Figure 5.11 shows that the Air Reserve Components have typically had lower rates of job and unit change than the other Reserve Components. About 13 percent of ANG members changed jobs each year since FY86 compared with 16, 15, 34, and 17 percent of ARNG, USAR, NR, and MCR members, respectively. The unit change rate is also about 13 percent in the ANG and is similarly lower than for the ARNG, USAR, NR, and MCR.

The AFR has had less turbulence than even the ANG, but unit change spiked to 25 percent in FY92. Since FY89, the job change rate has averaged only 7 percent in the AFR. These low rates of job change mean that the AFR has a much smaller retraining problem than the other Reserve Components, where job instability is more common.

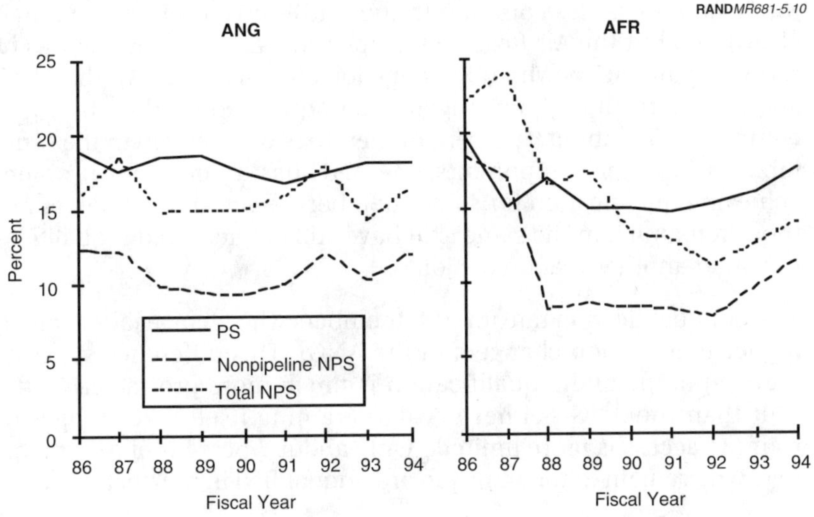

Figure 5.10—Percentage of Prior-Service and Nonprior-Service ANG and AFR Personnel Not Skill-Qualified, FY86–FY94

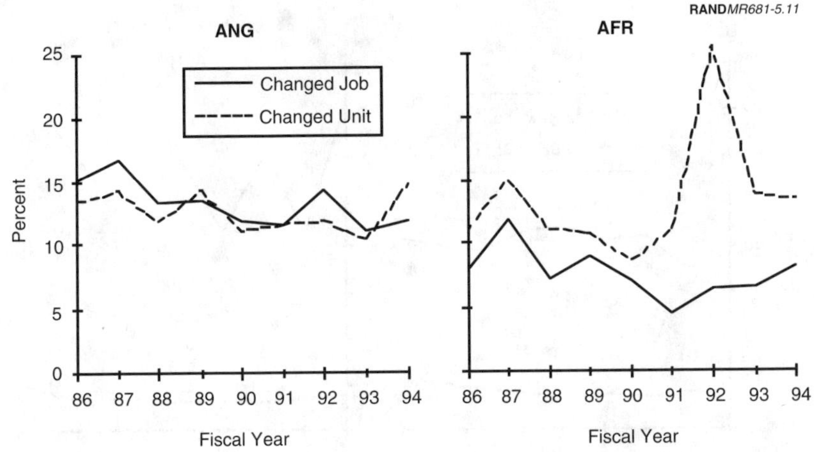

Figure 5.11—Percentage of ANG and AFR Personnel Changing Jobs or Units in Past Year, FY86–FY94

Job instability is less common in the Air Reserve Components than elsewhere, but the Air Reserve Components also face difficulties in retraining members who do change jobs (Figure 5.12). In the ANG, about 40 percent of job changers are unqualified for their new job, compared with about 9 percent of members who remain in the same job. As in other components, the ANG has a persistent problem achieving qualification for some members, since about 9 percent of those remaining in the same skill have still not achieved requalification after another year on the job.

The nonqualification rate for AFR members who change jobs is much higher than for job changers in the ANG. This difference suggests that retraining and requalification is much more protracted in the AFR than the ANG—either because training itself takes longer or training access is more limited. Only about 7 percent of AFR members who remain in the same job are unqualified in the next year.

Figure 5.13 shows that job change is much more likely for Air Reserve Component members who change units than for those remaining in the same unit. Intraunit job change is much less likely in the Air Reserve Components than elsewhere. Only about 4 or 5 percent of members switch jobs within the same Air Reserve Component unit.

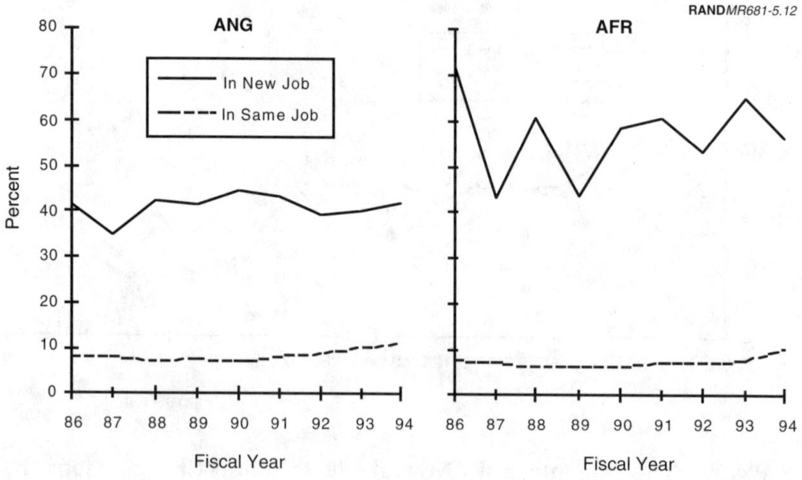

Figure 5.12—Percentage of ANG and AFR Personnel Not Skill-Qualified by Job Change Status in Past Year, FY86–FY94

The majority of unit changers have consistently changed jobs in the ANG. In most years, over 70 percent of members who changed units were assigned to different jobs in the new unit. In FY94, the movers had a job change rate of 49 percent, but it is unclear whether this represents a real improvement or a one-time aberration. Interunit mobility and job change are a substantial factor in explaining skill-qualification problems in the ANG.

Job change is much less likely for interunit moves in the AFR than in the ANG. The rate of job change among interunit transfers has been volatile but consistently less than 50 percent. In FY92, the job change rate fell to only 14 percent among movers, but the rate has since risen to 35 percent.

The Air Reserve Components have fewer skill-qualification problems than the other components, but about 17 percent of their members remain unqualified in their assigned skill in FY94. The lower non-qualification rates for the Air Reserve Components reflect their smaller training pipeline and lower rates of turbulence. As in other components, job changers have delays in requalifying in their new jobs, and most job changes are tied to members switching units.

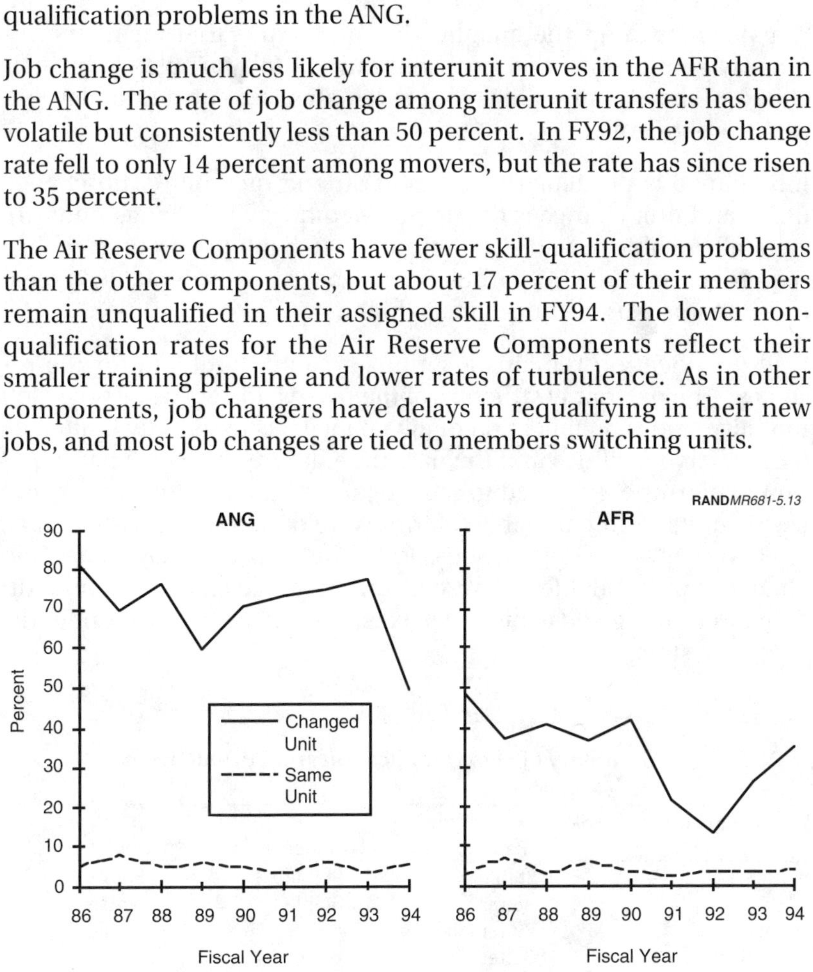

Figure 5.13—Percentage of ANG and AFR Personnel in New Jobs by Unit Change in Past Year, FY86–FY94

SUMMARY

Skill qualification remains a substantial problem for Selected Reserve units. Although qualification rates have improved in the USAR, NR, MCR, and AFR (see Table 5.1), all components have substantial shares of unit members who are unqualified in their assigned jobs.

A major reason for the qualification problem is that members frequently change jobs and need retraining. Job turbulence has declined in three components, but it remains at a substantial level in each component.

Job change is particularly common among members who change units, and unit change is common. Members who change units are generally unable to find a suitable job match in the new unit, so they require retraining. Unit turbulence has been relatively stable in most components, but the rates remain high.

Skill qualification remains a serious systemic problem for the reserves. The personnel structure of the reserve fosters widespread job mobility, and requalification of job changers is inherently limited by local reserve facilities and the part-time nature of reserve participation. Reforms are needed to reduce job turbulence both within and across units. Some possible reforms were outlined in Grissmer et al. (1994a), and are briefly discussed in the next chapter. When job change is unavoidable, the reserves should focus resources on individual retraining and avoid the pervasive delays that occur under the current system.

Table 5.1

Summary of Skill Qualification and Turbulence

Selected Reserve Component	Skill Qualification Rate	Job Turbulence	Unit Turbulence
ARNG	Stable	Stable	Stable
USAR	Better	Stable	Worse
NR	Better	Better	Stable
MCR	Better	Better	Better
ANG	Stable	Better	Stable
AFR	Better	Stable	Stable

Chapter Six

CONCLUSIONS AND FUTURE ISSUES

Our analysis of the more recent personnel indicators of the Selected Reserve Components suggests that the Reserve Components have improved in a number of respects, although there are clearly remaining areas of concern. The reserves are fielding a very senior, very experienced, and high-quality enlisted force and appear to have been successful in increasing their prior-service content over time (although still short of Title XI goals in some components). This increase results because the reserves have been able to take advantage of the considerably larger pool of losses created by the drawdown. The components have markedly increased their job match rates at entry for these new prior-service gains, and first-year attrition rates of these gains have also declined. Inventory attrition has remained remarkably stable over time—clearly, the ODS/S mobilization did not lead to the large outflow feared and predicted by some. Indeed, the attrition rate of PS individuals has remained stable or declined in some instances (although the attrition rate of reservists without prior service has increased). The skill-qualification rate has remained stable during the drawdown period and indicators of job turbulence and unit turbulence show modest improvement. The Selected Reserve Components can be justifiably proud of what they have accomplished in the last five years.

The analysis does, however, raise questions and concerns—some of immediate import and some that will need to be addressed in the near future.

INCREASING THE SUPPLY OF PS PERSONNEL

Prior-service personnel remain a critical resource for the Reserve Components because they enhance the experience base and reduce the training requirements of the reserves. The Reserve Components should investigate further initiatives to increase the affiliation rates of prior-service personnel to the reserves and to improve the utilization of prior-service skills. Several options merit attention.

- **Joint Active/Reserve Tours**. A new Army program formally links a two-year active-duty tour with a two-year tour in the Selected Reserves (Buddin and Roan, 1994). A key feature of the program is that Army College Fund monies were contingent on successful completion of the active-duty obligation *and* subsequent reserve participation. The RC affiliation rate for program participants was 80 percent, compared with about 40 percent for nonparticipants. Active/reserve job match was also improved under the program.
- **Supplemental Educational Benefits.** The reserves should consider new programs to provide extra educational benefits to prior-service personnel for affiliating with a reserve unit. Education monies have proven to be a valuable incentive for attracting recruits (Buddin and Roan, 1994) and ongoing research suggests that the college-bound group is a prime market for the Reserve Components. New educational benefits could be offered on a selective basis when vacancies exist in hard-to-fill skills or high-priority units.
- **Targeting Incentives.** New and reformed programs should place special emphasis on key well-defined reserve needs. Programs are more cost-effective if they are selectively structured to fill vacancies in early-deploying units or critical skills. Such incentives could be combined with others designed to keep individuals who are skill-qualified longer in the job, as discussed below.

IMPROVING SKILL-QUALIFICATION RATES

Skill qualification remains a serious problem for many Reserve Components. Some of the problem reflects the training pipeline for training nonprior-service personnel, when insufficient numbers of prior-service personnel are available to fill reserve vacancies. The primary cause of low qualification rates, however, is the high rate of job turbulence in the reserves and subsequent delays in members' requalifying in their new skill. We believe that substantive reforms are needed to reduce the rates of job and unit turbulence in the reserves. The reforms would change both the demand- and supply-side incentives to change jobs. On the demand side, the current system encourages units to compete both within and across components for new members. Such competition is frequently counterproductive to the reserves as a whole, since the old unit must recruit and train a new member and the new unit must generally retrain the transferred member in a new skill. On the supply side, we have seen that members frequently change units and we hypothesize that this is because the promotion prospects are better in the new unit (Buddin and Grissmer, 1994). Ongoing research in this area will help pinpoint the reasons for such turbulence and the reforms that might be effective in addressing this issue.

Job retraining and requalification procedures should be reassessed. When members change jobs, the reserves need options to speed requalification in the new job. The evidence shows that many members remain unqualified in their duty occupation for many months. The reserves face some inherent problems in retraining personnel locally part-time, but further research is needed to evaluate whether better planning and resource use might substantially reduce retraining time and enhance the skill qualification of reserve units.

To address the issue of skill and unit turbulence, our earlier report (Grissmer et al., 1994a) suggested the establishment of proficiency pay to reward experience and longevity in certain positions where experience is critical to job proficiency. Proficiency pay could be targeted toward higher-priority units and higher-priority skills. The amount of pay could vary by skill, grade, and amount of experience. The experience increments could take account of actual active, reserve, and related civilian experience. This additional pay for greater experience could be designed largely to offset the pay advantages of seeking promotion by switching to a new skill (as is currently the norm) and to give reservists greater incentives to stay in critical positions.

SUPPLY OF NONPRIOR-SERVICE INDIVIDUALS

A third issue that arises is the future supply of young reservists. It is clear that the near future will see a spate of retirements as the mid-career force becomes eligible for retirement, and that the reserve pool of PS individuals from which the reserves recruit will be considerably smaller because of reduced active force sizes. Both of these factors will increase the demand for nonprior-service individuals. However, there are a number of questions regarding the adequacy of the future supply of these young people.

First, the services report that they have fallen short of their recruiting goals in the last two years. If this is an indication of a decline in young people's interest in military careers and if this spills over to the reserve as well, there could be a decline in supply.

Second, the attrition rate for those without prior reserve service has increased over time. This may be deliberate, part of the reserve drawdown. If not, then it may prove troubling in the future and bears watching.

Third, the youth population is likely to become more ethnically diverse in the coming years and the propensities of these various ethnic groups—particularly recent immigrants—to enlist and remain in the reserves is largely unknown.

Fourth, quality may become an important issue. The military is likely to need more highly skilled people as we move to more technologically advanced methods of warfare; at the same time, there is increasing concern regarding the skills and aptitudes of future youth cohorts (this concern may be somewhat exaggerated—see Grissmer et al., 1994b). The overall question of supply, however, needs to be closely monitored, and policy options for increasing reserve supply—such as targeted enlistment and reenlistment bonuses, educational benefits, and shorter enlistment terms aimed at higher-quality recruits—need to be evaluated carefully.

Testing these policies on a limited basis is preferable to full-scale implementation, given the uncertainties of the future environment, force sizes, and force mix. Structured experimentation with many of these policies would help test their effectiveness and determine the best mix of new and old initiatives for addressing the issues raised above.

REFERENCES

Aspin, Les, *Report on the Bottom-Up Review,* Department of Defense, October 1993.

Brauner, Marygail K., and Glenn A. Gotz, *Manning Full-Time Positions in Support of the Selected Reserve,* Santa Monica, CA: RAND, R-4034-RA, 1991.

Brauner, Marygail K., Harry J. Thie, and Roger A. Brown, *Assessing the Structure and Mix of Future Active and Reserve Forces: Effectiveness of Total Force Policy During the Persian Gulf Conflict,* Santa Monica, CA: RAND, MR-132-OSD, 1992.

Buddin, Richard, and Carole E. Roan, *Assessment of Combined Active/Reserve Recruiting Programs,* Santa Monica, CA: RAND, MR-504-A, 1994.

Buddin, Richard J., and Stephen J. Kirin, *Army Reserve Component Accessions from Personnel Completing Their First Active-Duty Enlistment,* Santa Monica, CA: RAND, MR-258-A, 1994.

Buddin, Richard J., and David W. Grissmer, *Skill Qualification and Turbulence in the Army National Guard and Army Reserve,* Santa Monica, CA: RAND, MR-289-RA, 1994.

Department of Defense, *Reserve Component Program, Fiscal Year 1993: Report of the Reserve Forces Policy Board,* January 1994.

Greenwood, Michael J., "Immigrants and the U.S. Military: History and Prospects," in Mark J. Eitelberg and Stephen L. Mehay (eds.),

Marching Toward the 21st Century: Military Manpower and Recruiting, Westport, CT: Greenwood Press, 1994.

Grissmer, David W., Sheila Nataraj Kirby, Richard Buddin, Jennifer H. Kawata, Jerry M. Sollinger, and Stephanie Williamson, *Prior Service Personnel: A Potential Constraint on Increasing Reliance on the Reserve Forces,* Santa Monica, CA: RAND, MR-362-OSD, 1994a.

Grissmer, David W., Sheila Nataraj Kirby, Mark Berends, and Stephanie Williamson, *Student Achievement and the Changing American Family,* Santa Monica, CA: RAND, MR-488-LE, 1994b.

Grissmer, David W., and Sheila Nataraj Kirby, "A Total Force Perspective on Recruiting and Manning in the Years Ahead," in Mark J. Eitelberg and Stephen L. Mehay (eds.), *Marching Toward the 21st Century: Military Manpower and Recruiting,* Westport, CT: Greenwood Press, 1994.

Kirby, Sheila N., and David W. Grissmer, *Reassessing Enlisted Reserve Attrition: A Total Force Perspective,* Santa Monica, CA: RAND, N-3521-RA, 1993.

Marquis, M. Susan, and Sheila Nataraj Kirby, *Reserve Accessions Among Individuals with Prior Military Service: Supply and Skill Match,* Santa Monica, CA: RAND, R-3892-RA, 1989.

U.S. House of Representatives, *Report of the Committee on Armed Services, National Defense Authorization Act for Fiscal Year 1993,* H.R. 102-966, 1992.